Leaders of the People

Let us now praise famous men,
And our fathers that begat us.
The Lord manifested in them great glory,
Even his mighty power from the beginning.
Giving counsel by their understanding,
Such as have brought tidings in prophecies:
Leaders of the people by their counsels,
And by their understanding, men of learning
 for the people.

ECCLESIASTICUS

Leaders of the People

Josephine Kamm

Abelard – Schuman

London & New York

BOOKS BY THE SAME AUTHOR

For young people

African Challenge
He Went with Captain Cook
They Served the People
Men who Served Africa
Janet Carr: Journalist
Student Almoner
Sir Moses Montefiore

Biography

Daughter of the Desert:
a biography of Gertrude Bell
How Different from Us:
a biography of Miss Buss
and Miss Beale

FOR
CHARLES AND MARY
MONTEFIORE

AUTHOR'S NOTE

My grateful thanks are due to the Rev. Philip Cohen for helping me to plan this book and for reading the bulk of it in typescript. I should also like to thank Mr. Denzil Sebag-Montefiore for reading the chapter on Sir Moses Montefiore; Mrs. Ruth Berlak and Dr. Eva Reichmann for reading the chapter on Leo Baeck; and Mr. William Frankel for reading the chapters on Theodor Herzl and Chaim Weizmann.

I am indebted to Messrs. Hamish Hamilton Ltd. for permission to quote from *Trial and Error*, by Chaim Weizmann

CONTENTS

MOSES
The Law Giver

THE story of the Jewish people began some four thousand years ago. There was no civilized life then in Britain or America; but in Egypt and in the Babylonian Empire, which stretched from the Persian Gulf, through the whole of Asia and right on to the Mediterranean Sea, lived people who could read and write. They built temples, monuments and houses; they made musical instruments, trinkets, pottery and weapons of war. They worshipped many different gods and set idols (or images of their gods) in their temples and homes; and they believed that the kings who ruled them were sacred, and worshipped them as gods in life and death.

In the Babylonian Empire a man called Terah was born. According to the Bible, Terah was descended from Shem, son of Noah, who gave his name to the Semitic peoples. Terah, who lived in or near Ur, the chief city of Babylon, worshipped all the gods of his fellow citizens: but Terah had a son who turned away from the worship of many gods to the worship of one God, the God of Righteousness. Terah's son, who was called Abraham, left his home and his tribe nearly four thousand years ago in search of a place in which he could worship his God in peace. His journey took him to Canaan, a narrow mountainous strip of land between the desert and the shores of the Mediterranean.

The people of Canaan, like the peoples of Egypt and Babylon, worshipped idols: but Abraham taught his faith in the God of Righteousness to his own family, and through Abraham's family that faith took root and spread. Abraham's son Isaac was the father of Jacob; and Jacob—so the Bible tells us—received from God the name of Israel, which means "God fighteth." And so from Abraham to the long line of his descendants flowed faith in the one God. Abraham's great-grandchildren, the twelve sons of Jacob, became known as the Children of Israel (or the Israelites), a name which was borne by *their* descendants for century after century.

The Children of Israel continued to live in Canaan; but the Bible tells us how Joseph, Jacob's best-loved son, was sold as a slave by his jealous brothers and carried away to Egypt. Egypt was a mighty empire with a coastline on the Mediterranean, the sea which also formed one of the boundaries of Babylon. The Egyptians, under the rule of their powerful kings (or pharaohs, as they were called) were so sure of their own strength that they were ill-prepared to defend themselves. About the year 1730 before the present era Egypt was invaded by an army of warriors from Syria. These warriors, driving in horse-drawn chariots, were the Hyksos ("rulers of foreign lands"), a people, like the Children of Israel, of Semitic origin. In their thousands they overran unprotected Egypt, burning cities and temples, slaying many of the people, making slaves of the survivors. Then, having conquered the country, they made one of their own leaders pharaoh in place of the Egyptian ruler.

When Joseph was sold into slavery, Egypt was under the rule of the Hyksos. The story of Joseph, the brave and upright man who rose from slavery to become the king's Prime Minister, is a much loved Old Testament story. It was Joseph who had the granaries of Egypt filled with grain after each good harvest, so that when the harvests were poor the people had plenty to eat. But no such care for the future was taken beyond the frontiers of Egypt, and there the people were stricken by famine. It was then—so the Bible tells us—that Jacob sent his sons to buy corn in Egypt.

A painting found in the tomb of an Egyptian nobleman who died about the year 1900 BCE shows a wandering desert chieftain with his clan entering Egypt, and from this we can gain an idea of the appearance of the sons of Jacob and their families. In the picture the Egyptians wear nothing but white linen loin-cloths; but the visitors are dressed in red and blue striped kilts, and most of them wear as well an embroidered tunic fastened on one shoulder. The men have short pointed beards, while the women wear their thick dark hair loose, with a narrow fillet about their heads. The children wear shorts, and the youngest are carried on the back of an ass.

From the Bible we learn of Joseph's joy when he saw his brothers, of how he forgave their cruelty towards him and was reunited with his aged father. "And Pharaoh spake unto Joseph, saying, Thy father and thy brethren are come unto thee, in the best of the land make thy father and brethren to dwell: in the land of Goshen let them dwell." And so the Children of Israel settled in Goshen, a stretch of pastoral land between the Nile Delta and the Arabian Desert.

We do not know if this story happened exactly as the Bible tells it. Although the records left by the Egyptians describe how their country fell to the conquering Hyksos, they do not mention Joseph. We do know, however, that the Hyksos, who feared that one day the Egyptians would rise up against them, formed a vast armed camp to the east of the Nile Delta; and that they welcomed the arrival of a group of Hebrew wanderers of Semitic origin like themselves. The Hyksos thought that if the Hebrews settled in Goshen on the eastern frontier of Egypt they would form a barrier against an Egyptian rising. And so it seems very likely that the Hebrew wanderers who settled with their families and their herds and flocks in the rich pasture land of Goshen were indeed the brothers of Joseph.

Eventually—after about 150 years—the Egyptians banded themselves together, just as the Hyksos had feared, and drove the usurpers out of Egypt, never to return. The

Children of Israel, who had taken no part in the revolt, remained in Goshen, although, had they known what misery lay in store for them, they might well have fled.

The Egyptians had no love for the Hebrews. The Children of Israel, as the Egyptians knew, belonged to the same Semitic race as the Hyksos tyrants, and if they had been stronger and better armed might have fought on their side. But the Hebrews were not a warlike people. Some of them had learned the exquisite arts and crafts of the Egyptians and had become skilled in the working of gold and copper. Most of them, however, continued to live as shepherds. The Children of Israel, dwelling quietly in Goshen, had kept themselves apart from the Egyptians. They differed from them in religion and language, in race and occupation. The Egyptians feared them, perhaps because they were different; but also because beyond Goshen lived the lawless tribes of the desert, and they were afraid lest the Children of Israel and the desert tribes might one day join forces in an attack on their country.

Out of this fear grew oppression. The Israelites, who kept aloof from those around them, were an independent people, and the new Pharaoh determined to crush this spirit of independence by making them slaves. As he was starting to rebuild the cities which the Hyksos had destroyed and to strengthen their fortifications, it fitted in with his plans to use the Israelites as slaves. So now, instead of pasturing their sheep and goats on the plains of Goshen, they must dig clay from the river banks and provide straw to make bricks. If they failed to produce every day the number of bricks required of them, their Egyptian overseers punished them savagely. Too weak to rebel, too cowed to try to escape, the Israelites lived on in hopeless misery.

Still Pharaoh was not satisfied; and the Bible tells us that he resolved to exterminate the Hebrews by issuing an order that every baby boy born to a Hebrew mother should be drowned. Whether this order was actually issued seems doubtful, for why should Pharaoh seek to destroy his race of slaves ? But to the Hebrews the future of their children was dark whether they lived or died; and when a son was born to Jochebed, the wife of one of the slaves, there seemed little hope that he would grow up a free man.

Jochebed already had two children, a son called Aaron and a daughter, Miriam. When she saw them growing up to a life of wretchedness she made up her mind to save her baby, even if it meant parting from him. For three months she kept his birth a secret from all save her own family, and then, according to tradition, "she took for him an ark of bulrushes, and daubed it with slime and with pitch, and put the child therein; and she laid it in the flags by the river's brink."

Soon afterwards, the Bible story continues, Miriam, who was standing hidden in the rushes, saw Pharaoh's daughter come down to the River Nile and watched her lift the child from his cradle. It may sound strange to hear of a mother leaving her child in a cradle made of reeds or rushes: but an ancient inscription, which scholars have been able to read, tells how a great Semitic king, Sargon of Akkad, whose birth was also kept secret, was placed by *his* mother in a very similar cradle. The infant Sargon was rescued by a man who worked in the fields and brought up as a gardener until— says the inscription—he was chosen by a goddess to be king.

Jochebed's baby was rescued by a princess of Egypt. As she had no children of her own she decided to adopt him; and the name, Moses, which she gave him is probably derived from an Egyptian word which means "boy" or "son." It was the custom among the nobles of Egypt for children to be looked after by nurses outside their own family for the first few years of their life. Jochebed would have known of this custom and she must have told her daughter exactly what to do. When, therefore, Miriam realized that the princess meant to keep the baby she came forward timidly and offered to find him a nurse. The princess agreed, and Miriam went in search of her own mother. So it was that, unknown to his adopted mother, Moses spent his early childhood with his own family; and, realizing how soon she must give him up, Jochebed began to teach her son at a very early age the Hebrew customs and way of life and their ideas of right and wrong.

This story may not be accurate in all its details; but it is very probable that when his time with his mother was over, Moses was brought up in an aristocratic Egyptian family, not as a Hebrew but as an Egyptian nobleman. He was probably given a tutor (known in Egypt as a "father-nurse") who taught him to read and write; he would have learned more advanced subjects—such as mathematics—from the priests, who would also have told him of Egypt's many gods and goddesses. He would have gone, too, to the magicians to hear something of their ancient and mysterious arts.

As he grew to manhood Moses must have seen how different was his own carefree life from the life of the Hebrew slaves. They had enough to eat, it is true, for the Egyptians realized that well-fed workers could be made to do more than starving men; but they had been so harried and ill-treated that their lives no longer seemed worth living. And Moses, so the Bible tells us, "went out unto his brethren, and looked on their burdens."

When he became aware of the sufferings of the Hebrews, Moses felt drawn towards them, and because he was a free man enjoying all the privileges of rank and wealth he resolved to find some way of easing their burdens. Brooding on the problem one day as he walked among the hard-pressed slaves, he came on one of the Egyptian overseers "smiting an Hebrew, one of his brethren." Overcome with rage, Moses struck the Egyptian, who fell dead at his feet. In those days it was not considered a crime for a nobleman to kill an inferior. The blow had been struck in the heat of the moment, and the Egyptian had been treating the helpless slave most brutally. Yet Moses was well aware that Pharaoh would be angry that one of his officials had been killed for doing what he considered to be his duty. But over and above everything else Moses was overwhelmed with a feeling of guilt because he had slain a man: it was a feeling that he was to remember in the years to come.

Meanwhile, aware that Pharaoh might exact vengeance for

the deed, he decided on flight, and we next hear of him in Midian in the Arabian Desert. Here again he showed his eagerness to protect the weak from the strong. As he rested after his journey by the side of a well some young women approached to draw water for their flocks. But a group of shepherds, who had also come to draw water, refused to allow the women to go near the well. Moses sprang to his feet. He must have been a well-built man with an air of great authority about him, for singlehanded he drove the shepherds away. Before very long one of the young women he had helped became his wife. Her name was Zipporah, and when Moses married her he exchanged the luxurious life of an Egyptian nobleman for the simple life of a wandering shepherd.

During his years in the Arabian Desert Moses turned away from all that the Egyptian priests had taught him; and in the quiet and the solitude his belief in the One God, the God of Abraham, Isaac and Jacob, was deepened and strengthened. Gone was the stir of the city, with its temples and houses and its teeming, distracting life. Instead, the silence of the desert enveloped him and as far as his eye could see there was nothing but monotonous grey plateau, patched here and there with a welcome oasis of green. In this silence Moses had time to think and to pray; and, as his faith grew, he saw his God as the God of his fellow Hebrews, a God in whom they could safely put their trust, for He would "deliver them out of the hand of the Egyptians and . . . bring them unto a good land and a large, unto a land flowing with milk and honey." With his faith came the desire to help his persecuted people, and one day in a blinding flash came the knowledge that he must be the servant of God and the leader of God's people. For a time his sense of unworthiness fought with this conviction. "Who am I," he asked, "that I should go unto Pharaoh, and that I should bring forth the children of Israel out of Egypt ?" But conviction triumphed over doubt, and Moses made ready to return to Egypt and rescue the Hebrew slaves.

Although we do not know the year of Moses' birth or of

his return, historians believe that he quitted the Arabian Desert and journeyed to Egypt during the lifetime of the Pharaoh Rameses II, whose long reign of sixty-seven years lasted from 1301 to 1234 before the common era. Rameses II was known as "the Great." He was a warlike king, and a tireless builder of cities, temples and monuments to commemorate his victories; and he employed many slaves in the building of the cities which the Bible calls Pithom and Raamses. When Moses walked once more among his people he found them as brutally treated as ever. Still they toiled, without help and without hope; and when he began to speak to them of freedom they were too dazed and wretched to understand.

The years in the desert had changed Moses completely, and no one recognized the Hebrew leader as the young Egyptian nobleman who had fled from Pharaoh's wrath. It was not simply that he had grown older, that he was now a powerful, vigorous man, very young for his years. It was the spirit within him, the certainty that he was the appointed deliverer of his people, that had changed him. This knowledge gave him an air of authority, a power over men which even Pharaoh found hard to resist. For days Moses argued and pleaded with Pharaoh to release the Hebrew slaves, crying, "The Lord God of the Hebrews hath sent me unto thee, saying, Let my people go, that they may serve me in the wilderness."

Sometimes Pharaoh seemed on the point of relenting; but then, as though to taunt Moses with a display of his might, he gave orders that the slaves should be forced to work harder than ever. It was then, according to the Bible, that God through his servant Moses afflicted the Egyptians with a series of devastating plagues. These plagues and diseases were not new to the Egyptians, for they have been common in the Middle East for countless generations. But the Egyptians, like other peoples of their day, were very superstitious: they believed that floods and storms, diseases of men, cattle and crops were sent as a sign that the gods were angry. Their priests and magicians claimed magic powers;

and if a disease which was sweeping the country suddenly ceased, the people thought it was because the priests and magicians had interceded for them with the gods.

Yet now, as plague succeeded plague, the prayers and incantations of the priests and magicians failed to stop them. And what was more terrifying still, each disaster was heralded by a solemn warning from Moses. If Pharaoh would not release the slaves, cried Moses, then the waters of the Nile would be turned to blood. Haughtily Pharaoh refused: the people looked, and to their horror saw that the river was red indeed. Terrified, they cried that it was the God of the Hebrews who had caused the disaster. But Moses, who was familiar with the country and the people, must have known when he delivered his warning that the flood waters of the Nile were sometimes changed to a dark reddish-brown resembling blood by deposits from the lakes which fed them.

The plagues did not occur all at once; but before each Moses was at hand to prophesy what would happen. There was a plague of frogs, a plague of flies—both common enough happenings when the river was in flood; there were locusts which devoured the crops; a cattle disease which killed the animals. But if Moses knew in advance that these and other disasters were likely to occur, the superstitious Egyptians were filled with awe by the man himself, as well as by the plagues which he foretold. His commanding bearing, his air of great inner strength, and his utter conviction that he had been sent to release his people, all this set him apart from other men and above them. The Egyptians were forced to believe that the plagues had been sent by the God of the Hebrews and would not cease until the Hebrew slaves were liberated.

Still Pharaoh hesitated. Then a sandstorm broke out. Sandstorms occurred often enough, but this was one of hitherto unknown fury. It raged for three days: the air was dark with driven sand, which hid the sun, turning day into night. In the midst of the storm an epidemic started among the Egyptian children; and once more Moses was at

Pharaoh's side to prophesy both the storm and the sickness of the children.

During the days of darkness and terror a child—Pharaoh's eldest son—sickened and died. And so at length, in fear and desperation, Pharaoh sent for Moses and his elder brother, Aaron, crying, "Rise up, and get you forth from among my people, both ye and the children of Israel; and go serve the Lord, as ye have said."

Moses knew that Pharaoh was untrustworthy and that when the darkness lifted or the epidemic ceased he might change his mind. He therefore gave orders to the Israelites to make ready to leave without delay. By midnight their preparations had been made. Dressed ready for the journey, they ate a hasty meal of meat served with bitter herbs. Each man held a staff in his free hand, and on his back was a bundle containing dough which, had there been time, would have been baked into bread.

This was the Passover, "that night of the Lord to be observed of all the children of Israel in their generations." After they had eaten, the Israelites hurried to join Moses, and silently they set out on their journey. During the first day's march the dough which they carried was baked in the heat of the sun into flat, crisp cakes. These cakes are called *matzoth*, and to-day Jews all over the world eat them during the festival of Passover, which commemorates Israel's deliverance from captivity in Egypt.

The Exodus, as the departure from Egypt is called, took place about the year 1290 before the common era. Moses led his people in the direction of Canaan, the strip of country where Abraham had settled and where Jacob had lived with his family until the famine drove them to Egypt. The most direct route to Canaan would have taken them to Gaza on the coast; but the whole of this area was in the hands of the Philistines, a warlike people who would most certainly have resisted an Israelite invasion. It was probably in order to avoid open warfare that Moses chose the longer route through the desert. This way brought the Israelites by slow stages to the shores either of a marshy lake (no longer existing) called the "Reed" Sea, or close to the Red Sea, which washes the eastern coast of Egypt and is split at its northern end into two gulfs by the Peninsula of Sinai. As they pitched their tents for the night on the shores of the western gulf, the Gulf of Suez, the fugitives heard the distant thunder of chariots. They knew then that Pharaoh had broken his word and that the Egyptian army was pursuing them. Their plight was desperate. Before them lay the sea; behind, the enemy. As frightened people so often will, they turned to upbraid their leader, the man who was responsible for their flight. "It had been better for us to serve the Egyptians," they cried, "than that we should die in the wilderness."

Moses stood before them and with calm, encouraging words he sought to still their fears. "Fear ye not," he said, "stand still, and see the salvation of the Lord, which He will shew to you today." Then, as though in answer, the waters of the sea were whipped aside by a strong east wind, and the Israelites crossed over to the Peninsula on dry ground.

Pharaoh's army, approaching the shore, made ready to follow. But even as their ranks were mustered, the wind dropped: their chariots foundered in the sea, and every man and every horse was drowned.

To the fugitive Israelites their amazing escape was a sure sign that God was with them, and they raised their voices in praise and thankfulness. "Sing unto the Lord, for He hath triumphed gloriously; the horse and his rider hath He thrown into the sea." The Children of Israel lived in a barbarous age and so it was natural for them to sing a song of triumph at the disaster which had overwhelmed their enemies. They had not yet learned that the spirit of revenge has no part in the Jewish religion; and, as later Jewish teachers pointed out, despite the great crimes which the Egyptians had committed, their downfall was not a cause for rejoicing.

After their safe crossing of the Red Sea, Moses led his people south towards Mount Horeb, which is also known as Mount Sinai. It was here that during his sojourn in Midian he had first become aware of his great mission. In obedience to the command he had been given he had rescued his people from slavery. But the burden of leadership weighed heavily on him, for already the Israelites had forgotten their miraculous escape and were giving way to panic and despair. Although their lives had been made wretched by their Egyptian taskmasters, they looked back almost with longing to the security and the plentiful supply of food and water which had once been theirs. The dangers and hardships of a journey into the unknown terrified them, for they did not possess confidence in their leader. And Moses, understanding this, felt the need to strengthen and renew his own faith on Mount Horeb, the "Holy Mount."

The route which the Israelites followed had been used for centuries by the slave gangs which were sent to dig for copper and turquoise in the mines of the mountainous Sinai Peninsula. Whenever possible the limit of a day's march was from one well or waterhole to the next for, although those who journeyed carried water in goatskin bottles with them, they perished if they wandered far from a fresh supply. The description which the Bible gives of the journey is so detailed that scholars of our own age have been able to retrace it. The names of the oases by which the Israelites pitched their black tents spun and woven from goats' hair may have been changed, but the oases themselves still exist. The Bible tells us, for example, that at the start of the journey the Children of Israel wandered in the desert for three days without water until they came to a well of undrinkable water; and that soon after this they reached a fine oasis with "twelve wells and seventy palm trees." Forty-five miles from the northern tip of the Red Sea—a three-day march for people like the Israelites who were driving herds and flocks—there is a spring of water called by wandering Bedouin tribes "Ain Hawarah." The Bedouin do not camp by the spring, for the water is salty and full of sulphur. The ancient name for "Ain Hawarah" was "Marah." When, after three days without fresh water, the Israelites came to this spring they were disappointed. "And when they came to

Marah," says the Bible, "they could not drink of the waters
of Marah, for they were bitter."

A single day's march to the south of "Ain Hawarah" there
is today an oasis, with a number of wells shaded by palm
trees. This is the oasis with "twelve wells and seventy palm
trees" which is called in the Bible Elim, on the edge of the
Wilderness of Sin. At Elim the thirsty Israelites found not
only water but a plentiful supply of food; for "it came to
pass that at even the quails came up and covered the camp."

Now the Exodus happened in the springtime of the year,
the time in ancient days as well as today of bird migrations
from Africa to Europe. In the early months of the year
quails and other migrant birds fly across the Red Sea on
their journey to Europe. Worn out by their long flight they
alight in large numbers on the sea shore to rest a while before
going on; and they are so exhausted that it is very easy to
catch them.

The description in the Bible of the exhausted birds cover-
ing the camp is perfectly accurate. The Israelites knew
nothing of bird migrations. When they themselves were faint
with hunger the quails seemed to fall from the sky, and the
sudden arrival of this food was like a miracle. But more was
to follow. In the morning "when the dew that lay was gone
up, behold upon the face of the wilderness there lay a small
round thing, as small as the hoar frost on the ground." The
people asked their leader what these little beadlike objects
could be. "This," said Moses, "is the bread which the Lord
hath given you to eat." So the Children of Israel gathered a
supply of the white beads, which tasted like honey and which
they called "manna." And they continued to gather it month
after month, for each morning at daybreak the ground was
freshly covered.

Today, centuries later, manna can still be found in the
Sinai Peninsula, hanging in honey-sweet beads from grass,
stones and twigs. It is a kind of sap which comes out of
tamarisk trees and bushes when the bark is pierced by a
certain little insect. It falls to the ground and is gathered and
eaten by wandering desert tribes, just as the Israelites

gathered and ate it. But it is not surprising that the Israelites believed that this food, which appeared so miraculously every morning, had been sent by God to save them from starvation. For a while their trust in their leader was restored and they ceased their complaining. Yet time and time again, amidst the hardships of their wandering life, they were faithless to their God and disloyal to their leader. When Moses was with them they were steadied and strengthened by the power of the spirit within him, but he was not with them always. When he had gone up into the "Holy Mount" to renew his sense of guidance by prayer, the Children of Israel promptly forgot what he had taught them. Before they left Egypt, the superstitious Egyptians had pressed gold on them, thinking that with so rich an offering the Israelites might persuade their God to halt the plagues. Gold was of no use to God, and in the wilderness it was of no use to the Hebrews. When Moses was absent they took the gold and fashioned it into idols; and they worshipped these idols just as the Egyptians worshipped their gods.

When Moses returned to find what had happened, he seized the golden idols and flung them in the fire. Yet, angered as he was, he understood how the years of slavery had left the Israelites weak and unreliable, anxious to pray—as they had seen the Egyptians pray—to some god whose image they could see. The task he had set himself was to unite them in the worship of God and to weld them into a strong, free people.

The task took many years. At least once amidst the hardship and dangers of their wanderings the Israelites had to fight a battle. As the Bible puts it: "And all the congregation of the children of Israel journeyed from the Wilderness of Sin, after their journeys, according to the commandment of the Lord, and pitched at Rephidim. Then came Amalek and fought with Israel in Rephidim."

The scholars who have traced the ancient route followed by the Israelites discovered that ancient Rephidim is a fertile patch of land, shaded by palm trees and encircled by rocks. When the Amalekite people, who were accustomed to bring their flocks to drink and rest at the oasis, saw the Israelites approaching with *their* flocks they launched an attack. The two forces were equally matched and fighting continued throughout the day, first one side gaining the advantage, then the other. At length at sunset the Israelite force, under its captain, an able young follower of Moses named Joshua, gained the victory and the Amalekites fled.

To the Israelites Rephidim was simply a resting-place on their slow journey towards Canaan, a journey which the Bible says took forty years. Wherever they halted the black goats' hair tents were pitched, either for a single night or longer. The tents varied in size according to the wealth or position of the owner. Even the smallest had two compartments—one for the men of a family and for entertaining, the other for the women and children and for cooking. Instead of furniture there were mats of straw or goatskin; and the goats also provided the wanderers with milk.

At each resting-place, beneath Mount Sinai or at one or other of the water-holes, the Children of Israel camped by, Moses spoke of the future; and his steady faith and his confidence in the future of the Children of Israel enabled him, year in and year out, to guide the destinies of his people.

From his meditation on the mountain came those ideals which form the very roots of the Jewish religion and have inspired the whole world. "And Moses went up unto God," the Bible tells us. There, on the "Holy Mount," the great Commandments were made, with their opening like a clarion call: "I am the Lord thy God, which brought thee out of the land of Egypt, out of the house of bondage." The Children of Israel must put an end to the worship of idols: "Thou shalt not make unto thee any graven image, nor the likeness of any thing that is in heaven above, or that is in the earth beneath, or that is in the water under the earth." The fourth Commandment first gave the world the idea of a weekly day of rest: "Remember the Sabbath Day to keep it holy. Six days shalt thou labour, and do all thy work. But the seventh day is the Sabbath of the Lord thy God." No one must work on the day of rest, which must be a Sabbath for servant as well as master and even for cattle. In an age when so many men were slaves without any rights of their own, this Commandment showed understanding and sympathy.

Three thousand years ago the Commandments gave to the Children of Israel just and wise laws which men still revere today. They must respect their own parents, which meant, of course, caring for them when they were old. They must not steal. They must not be tempted to get their own way by bearing "false witness" (or giving wrong evidence) against any man. They should not try to obtain—or even want to obtain—anything belonging to anybody else. And in the Commandment, "Thou shalt do no murder," Moses must have recalled the sense of guilt which had haunted him since the day he smote and killed the Egyptian and fled into the desert to save his own life.

The real miracle of what occurred on Mount Sinai is this: that in an age of barbarity such a rule of life was born. One of the most dramatic passages in the Bible describes how Moses came down from the mountain, the stone tablets inscribed with the Commandments in his arms, his face alight with inspiration: "And when Aaron and all the Children of Israel saw Moses, behold, the skin of his face shone; and they were afraid to come nigh him."

The stone tablets were reverently placed in a tabernacle, a tent-like building specially made for them. They were enclosed in the Ark, a wooden box or chest, which stood behind drawn curtains in the farthest corner of the Tabernacle. Thus the Children of Israel learned to respect the great laws which have been theirs to this day.

The Ten Commandments were followed later by many other wise and far-sighted laws. These later laws were not made by Moses, but by the leaders who came after him and who had learned what he had taught. One of the finest condemned the practice of slavery at a time when it was taken for granted all over the East. Another impressed upon the Israelites that they should never seek revenge but, instead, should let the remembrance of their past sufferings make them generous towards others: "Thou shalt neither vex a stranger, nor oppress him, for ye were strangers in the land of Egypt."

During the lifetime of Moses, the Children of Israel had reached the last stage of their journey and made ready to cross the River Jordan and enter the land of Canaan. By the time they reached the southern border, Moses had transformed them from a straggling, frightened band of fugitives into a strong and vigorous people able to bear any hardship. During the forty years of wandering a whole new generation had grown up; and these young men had been trained for work which their fathers could not have attempted.

The Israelites were prepared to invade Canaan. The country was already occupied by a number of tribes. Some of these the Israelites fought and drove off: with others they made friends. The Canaanite peoples (as Abraham had discovered so long before) worshipped idols, offered human sacrifices to their gods and indulged in other cruel practices. The Israelites, who had learned from Moses to worship God and to lead a good life in a barbarous age, believed that everything that had happened to them had been according to God's will. So now they also believed that it was God's will that they should take land from the Canaanites. This was not as a reward to them, but as a punishment to the Canaanites for their wicked way of life.

Moses himself was not to enter this promised land. He was an old man now and very tired, and he knew that he had not much longer to live. So he sent the trusty Joshua with a small party of his followers to spy out the land. Joshua returned with reports of a wonderfully fertile country; and to prove it his men were carrying an immense cluster of grapes and baskets filled with figs and pomegranates.

The aged leader still had strength to climb a mountain, Mount Nebo (or Mount Pisgah as it is sometimes called); and there beneath him he saw the land spread out in all its promise. Then he turned to Joshua and handed over the leadership to him, "that the congregation of the Lord be not as sheep which have no shepherd."

It was Joshua and not Moses who led the people into

Canaan, for after the solemn handing-over of the leadership Moses, "the servant of the Lord," disappeared from sight to die alone. "No man," says the Bible, "knoweth of his sepulchre." There was no need for any one to know the spot where his body had lain: for like a beacon shining down the ages his life and his words will be remembered for ever.

ISAIAH OF JERUSALEM
(755 BCE - about 697)

THE Israelites who followed Joshua across the River Jordan captured the walled city of Jericho and invaded the hill country beyond. There were many bitter fights between the Israelites and the peoples of Canaan before the Israelites gained the advantage and divided the land among their tribes, which were named after the sons of Jacob. Even so, the Canaanite tribes had not been decisively beaten, and while some of them fled others remained to harry the Israelite settlers. Chief among these were the Philistines, who lived along the coastline of the Mediterranean, their eastern frontier bordering on Israelite territory. In the skirmishes and battles which broke out, the Philistines were often victorious, and they oppressed the Israelites harshly.

After Joshua's death the Children of Israel were governed by a number of courageous leaders (or Judges). Samuel, the last and the most famous of these Judges, united his people, as Moses had sought to unite them, in the worship of the One God; and through this religious unity they achieved strength.

Samuel was a man who, like Moses, needed peace and solitude. But the Children of Israel wanted a leader who would be with them at all times and would act as a general to their forces, and they persuaded Samuel to appoint a king over them. The choice fell on Saul of the tribe of Benjamin. Saul, brilliant but unstable, became King of Israel about the year 1030 B C E. He mustered the people and led them against their enemies; but the Israelite forces were inferior to those of the Philistines. Everyone knows the story of the shepherd boy, David, who killed the Philistine champion Goliath in single combat and so gained a victory for the Israelites. Everyone knows of Saul's jealous persecution of the young hero, and of how he himself in the end was hopelessly defeated by the Philistines and died by his own sword rather than face capture.

David, son of Jesse of Bethlehem, succeeded Saul as King of Israel and became the greatest of the Kings. He united the tribes in a firm alliance, made the city of Jerusalem his capital, and defeated all his enemies.

Jerusalem and the other walled cities of Old Testament times looked rather like castles. For safety's sake they were built on hilltops which gave the sentries a good view of an approaching enemy. They were guarded by double gates, and their solid walls, built of stone and brick, followed the irregular outlines of the hill.

To his son, Solomon, David bequeathed an empire made up of two separate but united kingdoms, Israel and Judah. King Solomon, known as "the wise," built a magnificent Temple in Jerusalem; and in the farthest corner, hidden by a curtain, he set the Holy of Holies—the Ark containing the stone tablets of the Law, which the Children of Israel had carried with them wherever they went. Solomon was not as great a king as his father; and after his death there was strife between Israel and Judah. The two kingdoms then divided, each under its own king, and instead of friendship between them there was rivalry. Israel, the northern kingdom, was the more important of the two, for there lived ten of the twelve Israelite tribes. Judah, to the south, with Jerusalem, its capital, contained only the tribes of Judah and Benjamin, who had remained loyal to David in the days of his persecution by Saul.

The two separate states were never as powerful as they

had been as parts of a single kingdom, and neither was strong enough to withstand the might of foreign invaders. They were further weakened by a slackening of the faith which had once united them; by a disregard of the Commandments, and a relapse into the worship of idols.

In both kingdoms there were wise men who fought against these evils, denounced the people for their wrong-doings, and preached to them of their duty to their God and to their fellow men. These men were the prophets, or messengers of God. With the utmost courage they spoke of wrongdoing and duty, not only to the ordinary people, but to their kings, who could put them to death. They prophesied coming disaster, and they implored their hearers to return to the worship of God and to obey His laws before it was too late.

It was in the year 737 BCE, some two hundred years after the separation of the two kingdoms, that a young man of about eighteen went into the Temple which King Solomon had built. He had come—as he came very often—to pray for the people of the little kingdom of Judah, whose King, Uzziah, had recently died. The young man's name was Isaiah. Although we do not know if he was related to King Uzziah, he was almost certainly of noble birth and had been brought up in court circles on friendly terms with the royal family. No details of his childhood have come down to us, but we do know that he could read and write and that he had learned enough of his country's affairs to take a keen interest in its welfare.

We can picture the young man, then, dressed in long robes and with the elaborately curled hair and beard of the time, as he passed through the great Outer Court of the Temple into the Inner Court, with its inlaid cedarwood walls and its fine golden candlesticks. Before the gold curtains which concealed the Holy of Holies Isaiah stood, wrapped in deep thought. He had the same burning faith in God which had inspired Moses and which inspired every one of the prophets; and now, as he waited, he felt his faith swell within him. He neither moved nor prayed aloud, yet his soul—his inner being—was filled with a vision which came to him alone. As he waited expectantly the heavy folds of the curtains appeared to move, changing before his eyes into the drapery of a robe; and the robe covered the form of God Himself seated on a lofty throne. Around the throne the young man seemed to see a group of fiery angels, their faces veiled by their wings, their voices thundering: "Holy, holy, holy, is the Lord of hosts: the whole earth is full of His glory."

It was as though the thunder of the angels' voices caused the pillars of the Temple to tremble and the very foundations of the building to shake; and Isaiah's eyes were suddenly blinded by heavy smoke which filled the Inner Court. He felt then that he was in the very presence of God, and the knowledge filled him with a sense of his unworthiness. Nearly five hundred years earlier this same feeling of unworthiness had caused Moses to cry: "Who am I that I should go unto Pharaoh, and that I should bring forth the children of Israel out of Egypt ?" Yet Moses had been driven by a force within stronger than himself, and so was Isaiah. The same force inspired each one of the prophets, wiping out their sense of unworthiness, impelling them to answer a call. It was like a burning which never consumed them, yet drove them to speak, whatever the consequences.

So now, Isaiah seemed to hear deep within his soul the voice of God demanding: "Whom shall I send, and who will go for us ?" And then, without a moment's hesitation, Isaiah answered: "Here am I: send me." He made his offer of service impulsively, carried away by the magnificence of his vision. When he realized what his task was to be, he may well have been daunted, but he did not draw back. He learned that he was to be the guide and teacher of the people of Judah: he would prophesy, but his words would not be believed: he would teach, and the people would hold up his words to scorn. When he begged to know how long his message must fall on unresponsive ears he received the frightening reply: "Until the cities be wasted without inhabitant, and the houses without man, and the land be utterly desolate."

In the scene of despair which these words evoked there was a single gleam of hope. "But yet in it there shall be a tenth, and it shall return." In the years to come Isaiah was often to be downcast and discouraged by his inability to make the people believe how urgent was his message; but always he found comfort in this promise of salvation for the remnant of a nation which he knew to be doomed to destruction.

So Isaiah exchanged his robes for the simple goatskin garment worn by the wandering prophets, and his life of ease for one of hardship. Very little is known about him; but his love of God, his concern for his people, are beautifully revealed in the first thirty-nine chapters of the Old Testament book which bears his name. His teaching life lasted for more than forty years, years of unrest and trouble during which he toiled in vain to persuade the people to mend their ways. We know that he was married, and because he speaks of his wife as a prophetess it is clear that she believed in the truth of his message and encouraged him in the days of despondency. There were two sons of the marriage, and their names were chosen to convey a special meaning. The younger was called Maher-shal-al-hash-baz, a name to impress on the people the fate which would overtake them if they refused to lead better lives, for translated it reads: "Speed, spoil, haste, destruction." But the elder was called Shear-jashub, which means, "the remnant will return," and reflects Isaiah's faith that God would surely redeem a tenth of the stricken population.

While our knowledge of the events of Isaiah's life is so small (we do not even know when he died), his writings give us a clear picture of a man of the greatest courage. He was stern yet kindly; and in his sternest words we can sense his love for his people and for his city, a love so deep that he is known to us as Isaiah of Jerusalem. He had first shown his courage when he offered himself in the Temple and held to his word even when he knew that his message must go unheeded. And he proved it again and again when, without a thought for his own safety, he upbraided the people—from the humblest in the land to the King himself—exhorting

c

them to do their duty to God and to one another. In addition to his other qualities he had an immense fund of what today we should call sound common sense, a statesman's understanding of Judah's problems, and a general's knowledge of the military dangers which threatened the kingdom. He realized that Judah and the northern kingdom Israel were little more than buffer states existing precariously between three mighty empires, Assyria, Egypt and Syria; and the advice he gave to the Kings of Judah was that it would be wiser to remain neutral than to seek to form an alliance with any one of these powers against the others. The Kings of Judah, he said, should put their trust in God and not in man.

Isaiah had begun his work, as he himself tells us, "in the year that King Uzziah died." Uzziah had been a staunch believer in God—unlike some of the other Kings of Judah who relapsed into the worship of idols. He had been a good ruler and had done much to build up the trade and agriculture of his kingdom and to strengthen its defences. For the last years of his life he was stricken by leprosy, the dreadful disease so common in the East, and the kingdom had been ruled in his name by his son, Jotham, who succeeded him when he died. Under Jotham, too, the country prospered; but the people used this prosperity simply as an excuse for idleness and extravagance.

Towards the end of Jotham's reign the King of Israel and the King of nearby Syria decided to form an alliance against the formidable empire of Assyria. They hoped that if all the smaller states banded together they would be able to withstand a possible invasion by the armies of Assyria; and so they invited Jotham to join them. This was just what Isaiah had feared might happen, but much to his relief Jotham refused the invitation. Angered by his refusal, the Kings of Israel and Syria tried to intimidate him by sending out small armed bands to raid the isolated villages in the Judean hills. Jotham persisted in his refusal. But Jotham died, and his successor, his son Ahaz, was a weak man, easily frightened by a display of power. The Kings of Israel and Syria, who must have been well aware of this, launched a full-scale attack on Judah, captured a number of defended cities and set siege to the capital itself.

Unable to make up his mind what course to take, Ahaz was considering an appeal for help to mighty Assyria, whose massive armies could easily crush the combined forces of Israel and Syria. He was pondering this plan one day as he inspected the fortifications of the city, probably thinking of the actual wording of the appeal, when he suddenly encountered Isaiah with his small son Shear-jashub. The meeting was no accident, for Isaiah was on his way to the palace to ask for an audience with the King. He suspected what Ahaz had in mind, and was anxious to prevent it. The King of Assyria, as Isaiah guessed, would not refuse to send help to Judah; but he would do so only on condition that Judah surrendered her independence and became a slave-state of the Assyrian Empire. The Prophet did not share the King's fears that the whole of Judah would be overrun: he believed that God would deliver Judah from the Kings of Syria and Israel, "those smoking firebrands," as he called them. And so he advised faith in God, and implored Ahaz not to consider asking help from Assyria. Ahaz listened to his words, but he put no trust in them.

Then Isaiah offered him a sign that God alone could save Judah, any sign he liked to ask. But Ahaz, who had already decided to appeal to the King of Assyria, refused. Then, angered by Ahaz's stubborn attitude, Isaiah cried aloud: "The Lord Himself shall give you a sign." A young woman would have a son, he said, whom she would call Immanuel (meaning "God with us"). "Butter and honey shall he eat when he knoweth to refuse the evil and choose the good. For, before the child shall know how to refuse the evil and choose the good the land whose two kings thou abhorrest shall be forsaken."

Over the centuries people have argued and disputed about this saying. Put in simple terms, the explanation is this: by the time a child, as yet unborn, has learned to distinguish between wholesome food and harmful—that is, while he is still young—the Kings of Israel and Syria would be defeated and the threat to Judah removed. And the child's name—Immanuel—is proof that, unlike Ahaz, his mother believed that God would save her country. This is the explanation which Jews have always accepted. But to very many Christians the saying has a much more profound meaning, although a growing number of Christian scholars disagree with it. To the majority of Christians, Isaiah was not speaking merely of a short space of time: he was prophesying the birth of Jesus. In this verse, and in other verses in the Book of Isaiah in which the Prophet speaks of the Prince of Peace, the perfect King, who should be descended (as were all the Kings of Judah) from Jesse, the father of David, they see prophecies which were borne out in the life of Jesus.

Whatever the division of thought which Isaiah's words have brought about, Ahaz, the man to whom they were spoken, refused to accept them as a sign that God alone could preserve Judah from the armies of Syria and Israel. Instead, he sent messengers to beg for armed help from the powerful King of Assyria. The King listened to their plea and promised to send help; but he promised it on the very condition that Isaiah had feared—that Judah should surrender her independence and become a vassal state to Assyria.

The messengers of Ahaz accepted the Assyrian terms. The Assyrian armies were ordered to march against Syria and Israel; and so strong were they, and so well equipped with weapons and chariots, that they gained an overwhelming victory. They laid waste the kingdom of Israel, destroyed and looted its cities, and led away the entire population to death or lifelong captivity. So complete was the destruction that Israel, for so long the more important of the two Hebrew kingdoms, vanished for ever. Israel had existed for about 215 years, from 937 to 722 BCE. The kingdom of Judah was to survive for a further 136 years, until 586 BCE. And when, as we shall see, Judah, too, was overrun and her people taken captive, a remnant did in fact survive—as Isaiah had prophesied—to become the ancestors of the Jewish peoples of today. But while the survivors were in fact Judeans—men and women from Judah—the name "Judah" has been discarded, and the name "Israel," which was first given to Jacob, is the name which has lived on.

Meanwhile, the mighty empire of Assyria, which had conquered Israel and Syria, had also subdued Judah, and Ahaz adopted Assyrian customs and worshipped Assyria's gods. It is true that there was an interval of peace, but only at the price of Judah's independence and the heavy tribute which the people were forced to pay every year to the King of Assyria. So irksome did the burden become that some of the nobles of Judah began to plot an alliance with the third of the great powers, Egypt.

When Isaiah learned of this he went straight to the new King, Hezekiah, who had recently succeeded his father Ahaz. The Prophet implored Hezekiah, as he had implored his father, to keep the country free from foreign entanglements, to put his trust in God. Once again his words went unheeded, and despairingly he cried: "The vision of all is become unto you as the words of a book that is sealed." The King wanted an Egyptian alliance: and Isaiah, lamenting that Judah had "made a covenant with death," walked among the people barefoot, clad only in the single cloth worn by prisoners of war, as a sign of what their fate would be.

Isaiah was convinced that Egypt could not prevail against Assyria. He was right, for the Egyptian army suffered a series of crushing defeats. Some idea of the power of the Assyrian Empire can be gained from a series of sculptures discovered about a hundred years ago, which depict scenes from the reign of the powerful King Sennacherib, who ruled from 705 to 681 BCE. There were more than seventy rooms in the royal palace at Nineveh, and they were lined with stone slabs carved with battle scenes and sieges, with processions of slaves and horses, and with scenes showing the building of the palace and the two great winged bulls sculptured in stone which stood before it. Engraved on a cylinder of baked clay was the proud King's description of himself: the great and mighty King, the King of the Universe, the lover of justice, the perfect hero, the mighty man who quells the rebel and strikes the wicked with his thunder-bolts. In the British Museum in London, among the relics of Sennacherib's reign, there is a magnificent carving of the King. He is seated on his throne, receiving prisoners of war, who are chained together and guarded by Assyrian soldiers.

The Assyrian war machine had three arms—cavalry, infantry and chariots. The soldiers carried shields and wore helmets and suits of mail. They fought with swords, spears, slings and bows and arrows. But their most dreaded weapon was the battering-ram, a heavy wood and metal beam mounted on a siege engine. The siege engine, the ancestor of the modern tank, was worked by a crew of soldiers and could shatter the masonry of a city's walls. The very thought of it struck terror into the hearts of Assyria's enemies.

When King Hezekiah of Judah realized that his tiny country would be overrun as the Assyrian armies passed in their triumphant progress to Egypt, he sent in terror for Isaiah, who had warned him what would happen. Although Isaiah was well aware of Judah's weakness he had no fear of the consequences. God, he told the King, would not let Jerusalem fall to Sennacherib: "Behold, I will send a blast upon him and he shall hear a rumour, and return to his own land: and I will cause him to fall by the sword in his own land."

This time Hezekiah, an upright man, very different from his father Ahaz, believed what Isaiah said and took heart. He did not waver when one by one the cities of Judah capitulated, nor when Sennacherib sent an ambassador to demand the surrender of Jerusalem. "Thus saith the King," cried the ambassador; "let not Hezekiah deceive you: for he shall not be able to deliver you. . . . Hath any of the gods of the nations delivered his land out of the hand of the King of Assyria?"

When he heard this arrogant boast Hezekiah prayed to God for strength; and he sent a brave and defiant answer to Sennacherib. To those who awaited the approach of the massed Assyrian armies the fate of Jerusalem must have seemed certain. And yet the city was spared. As the

Assyrians encamped some distance from the city, an epidemic of swift-killing plague broke out, and within a few hours thousands of men lay dead. As the Bible describes the disaster: "Then the angel of the Lord went forth, and smote in the camp of the Assyrians a hundred and four score and five thousand: and when they arose early in the morning, behold, they were all dead corpses."

The survivors turned in panic and fled back to their own country: "So Sennacherib King of Assyria departed, and went and returned, and dwelt in Nineveh." Sennacherib never came back, and twenty years later this proud and mighty king was murdered by his own sons as he prayed in the temple of his gods.

After the dramatic flight of Sennacherib's broken armies we hear no more of the prophet Isaiah, for the remaining chapters in the Book which bears his name refer not to him but to another man altogether. But although we know nothing of the last years of Isaiah's life, his record as faithful adviser and reformer, is with us for all time. To the last he remained firm in his belief that although God would judge and condemn Judah, for the faithful remnant a new and better age was in store: "and the remnant that is escaped of the house of Judah shall again take root downward, and bear fruit upward: For out of Jerusalem shall go forth a remnant, and they that escape out of Mount Zion: the zeal of the Lord of hosts shall do this." He spoke, too, of that final age of peace—an age which we still long for today—when the people "shall beat their swords into ploughshares, and their spears into pruning hooks; nation shall not lift up sword against nation, neither shall they learn war any more."

JUDAS MACCABEUS
(d. 160 B C E)
The Hero of Judea

ALTHOUGH the menace of Assyria had been lifted from Judah, another great military empire, Babylon, had come into being to cast covetous eyes on the little kingdom. In 587 B C E the Babylonian armies set siege to Jerusalem. For eighteen months the defenders held out heroically. But at length, beaten by famine and an epidemic of disease which added to the horrors of the siege, they surrendered.

Jerusalem was then utterly destroyed. The Temple, the royal palace and the chief buildings were burned to the ground, and the fortifications torn down. The chief priest and the other leaders were slain, and many of the people carried into captivity in Babylon. Just a very few—shepherds or peasants—probably remained in Judah, all that was left of the twelve tribes of the Children of Israel who had entered the Promised Land five hundred years before. The history of Judah was at an end: the Children of Israel were scattered.

With the dispersal of the tribes, the names " Israelite " and "Children of Israel" ceased to be used. Instead, the people were called Jehudahites—or Jews; and they have been called Jews ever since. The Jews who were taken captive to Babylon were not harshly treated, and some of them settled down happily enough. Others grieved endlessly for their lost country, for Jerusalem and the Temple which had been destroyed. We can read the lament of these unhappy exiles in Psalm 137: "By the rivers of Babylon, there we sat down, yea, we wept, when we remembered Zion."

The exile lasted for nearly fifty years, long enough for the mourners to die and for a whole new generation of Jews to grow up. It might have continued much longer had it not been for a ruler who was kind and merciful. This man was Cyrus, King of Persia, whose mother had been a Babylonian princess. Cyrus defeated the Babylonian army in battle in 539 B C E. He entered Babylon at the head of his troops as a conqueror; but he did not behave like other conquerors of his day, who destroyed cities and killed the people or carried them off into slavery. Cyrus ordered no executions, no destruction. He came in peace; and his troops, instead of burning and killing, wandered peacefully about the country-side. On a clay tablet which was discovered in modern times there is a written description of this and of how the conqueror declared, "I let no man be afraid."

Cyrus set himself—as all wise rulers have done—to make life better for the people; and when he saw so many Jews mourning for Jerusalem he gave them permission to go back to their native land. Those Jews who preferred it remained in Babylon. But to the rest, the thought of returning to Jerusalem was like a wonderful dream come true. They set out on the journey from Babylon to Jerusalem laden with gifts, for Cyrus had returned to them the gold and silver vessels which the Babylonians had stolen from the Temple as spoil, and many gifts besides.

The first work to which the returning exiles set their hands was the rebuilding of the Temple. It was a task which took many years. The work of destruction had been very thorough; and Jerusalem was surrounded by enemies, alien tribes who did their utmost to hinder the builders. As soon as the ruins had been cleared away an altar to God was set up and the foundations of the new Temple laid; and while the building was slowly erected, the fortifications of the city were being rebuilt. The Jews lived dangerously, and it is said that those of them who were employed on the fortifications had to carry a sword in one hand and a builder's tool in the other.

While the work was in progress Ezra, who was a priest and a scribe, came to Jerusalem from Babylon bringing with him a number of priests. Every day Ezra read aloud to the people a portion of the Book of the Law of Moses; and he set himself the task of re-uniting the people in the worship of God and obedience to the Law.

In the meantime, another Jew—Nehemiah—was in charge of the rebuilding of the fortifications of Jerusalem and the other cities which the Babylonians had destroyed. King Cyrus of Persia had died a few years after his peaceful conquest of Babylon; and Nehemiah was cup-bearer to his successor. When the King realized how deep was Nehemiah's longing to join his people he gave him permission to pay two long visits to Jerusalem, the second visit in 432 BCE. But Nehemiah was not only a builder: he was also a law-maker, and he is remembered for many wise reforms.

Between them, Ezra and Nehemiah welded the people once more into a strong religious community. The country (which was now called Judea) enjoyed many years of peace as a province of Persia.

Then a new conqueror arose, Alexander the Great, the Greek King of Macedon, who was born in 356 BCE. Alexander, a brilliant soldier, overthrew the Persian king, captured and occupied all the cities along the Mediterranean coast, and conquered Egypt. After a series of staggering victories the conqueror died in Babylon at the age of thirty-three, leaving to his successors an immense new empire.

Alexander's empire was carved up after his death into several different parts; and the province of Judea, which had come to Alexander with the conquest of Persia, became a prize which was fought for by Egypt and Syria. Eventually, more than a hundred years later, the prize went to Syria, whose king was Antiochus IV.

Although Alexander the Great had lived so short a time the influence of Greece and the Greek way of life and worship was very powerful and very widespread. The Jews did not worship the Greek gods, but some of them had adopted Greek customs. Some, too, had left Judea to settle in the surrounding countries, and from time to time they were joined by relatives and friends. So once again the Jews were dispersed, but this time they went of their own free will. Yet in Jerusalem and elsewhere there remained groups of pious Jews who clung to their own laws and their own way of life.

The Jews did not form a nation and they had no king. The most important man among them was the High Priest, who was anointed with oil as the kings had been, and who was looked upon as their leader.

Antiochus IV of Syria was known as Antiochus Epiphanes, a name meaning "the God who reveals himself." Antiochus was a harsh ruler who set himself to crush any sign of independence among the Jews. He did not imagine that this would be difficult, for the Jews, who were weak in arms and armed men, were further weakened by quarrels among themselves. The quarrels were between the strictly loyal Jews and those Jews who still preferred the Greek way of life. There was rivalry, too, for the sacred office of High Priest. This rivalry led to civil war, and gave Antiochus the excuse he wanted to intervene, which, as overlord, he believed he had a perfect right to do.

In 169 BCE Antiochus attacked Jerusalem, forced an entry into the city, and massacred the people, men and women, old and young alike. Then, entering the Temple, he gave orders for the golden altar, the candelabra and all the vessels of gold and silver to be removed.

Antiochus then issued a decree, and sent it forth to every city in Judea, which forbade the Jews to worship God and ordered them to build altars and offer sacrifices to the Greek gods. The Jews were also forbidden to observe the Sabbath and the festivals or to keep the laws about the eating of unclean food. Officials were appointed to see that the Jews obeyed; and disobedience was punished with death. Fear led some of the Jews to do as they were ordered; but many more, revolted by the savage cruelty of the tyrant and determined to keep their faith, fled into hiding in the caves and ravines of the Judean mountains.

· The officials appointed by Antiochus went from city to city, destroying the synagogues, tearing to pieces and burning the scrolls of the Law. These senseless outrages only served to unite the people, and their resistance was encouraged by a very strict religious sect known as the Chassidim. Most of the Chassidim had gone into hiding, but now they left their hiding-place to rally the people and implore them to face death rather than submit. When the Chassidim returned to their caves they were followed by hundreds of Jews who had bravely decided to seek refuge with them.

The hiding-place the Chassidim had chosen was a safe one in the caves. But some traitor revealed it to the enemy; and one morning the fugitives awoke to see a band of armed men approaching. They offered no resistance, for the attack had been timed for the Sabbath, and the Chassidim refused to profane the day by taking up arms. They would not even lift a stone to close the entrance to the caves; and so they perished, every man, woman and child.

This was a heroic action: yet, if all the Jews in Judea had followed the example of the pious Chassidim, they would soon have been wiped out. But the massacre of these innocent people had left them leaderless; and, frightened by threats, they might have been driven to submit, had not new leaders arisen at the moment of their greatest danger.

These new leaders were a father and his five sons who belonged to the family of the Hasmonæans, or Maccabees as they are sometimes called. The father was an aged priest named Mattathias, who had fled from Jerusalem after the sack of the Temple and had settled in Modin, a mountain village between Jerusalem and the sea. The story of Mattathias and his sons is told in the Apocrypha (the collection of historical and religious writings which is not included in the Hebrew Bible). It was also related by the first important Jewish historian, Flavius Josephus, who was born about a hundred years after the events took place. Later writers have retold the story; and while the outlines are true, the details may have been exaggerated.

Mattathias rallied the people of Modin, begging them to die fighting rather than obey Antiochus' decree. Soon, as he had expected, a Syrian official entered Modin at the head of a party of armed men. When the official ordered the people of Modin to renounce their religion and to worship the Greek gods Mattathias appeared before him, flanked by his five stalwart sons. Commanded to set an example to his people, Mattathias answered bravely: "If all the people in the kingdom obeyed the order of the monarch, to depart from the faith of their fathers, I and my sons would abide by the Covenant of our forefathers."

The people were deeply moved by these brave words; but one man, terrified that they would be followed by a massacre, approached the altar, promising to sacrifice to Zeus, father of the Greek gods. Overcome with anger, Mattathias seized the man as he stood before the altar and killed him with his bare hands. Then his sons, armed with long knives, fell upon the Syrian official and his troops and slew every one of them. Afterwards they destroyed the altar which had been profaned by the sacrifice and by the slaughter.

Mattathias cried aloud to the people: "Whoever is a zealous defender of the Law, and whoever wishes to support the Covenant, follow me." The people did not hesitate: the entire population of Modin followed the aged priest and his five sons to the refuge they had chosen in the mountains of Ephraim. There they were joined by other Jews fleeing from persecution, who saw in Mattathias and his sons a shield against oppression.

The priest did not hide from his people that they would have to fight, nor that if they were defeated they would be cruelly put to death. And warned by the fate of the Chassidim he and his sons decided that if they were attacked on the Sabbath they would take up arms and fight. Mattathias and his sons inspired their followers with some of their own courage and confidence. But they were few in number in comparison with the enemy; and before long the timid and the frightened were deserting to join the Syrians or find hiding-places of their own. With so small a number of fighting men at his disposal, Mattathias avoided open warfare and, instead, led a number of daring raids. He and his sons knew every inch of the country; and every now and then, with a small band of picked followers, they would enter a town, destroy the temples and altars at which the Greek gods were worshipped, and then retire swiftly to their mountain stronghold. If these raids did no damage to enemy troops, they showed the Syrians and the Jews who lived under Syrian rule that the worship of the One God was still a living faith.

But Mattathias, who had planned his raids well, was growing very feeble. When he knew that he was dying he called his followers about him to choose a new leader. There was only one difficulty in the choice—which of his valiant sons would serve the people best ? After much deliberation the dying man chose the greatest thinker among them—whose name was Simon—to be adviser: but the real leader was to be Judas—whose surname "Maccabeus" means "the Hammer." "Do you then esteem Simon as your father," Mattathias told his people (according to the historian Josephus), "because he is a man of extraordinary prudence. Take Maccabeus for the general of your army, because of his courage and strength." And with his last breath the old man begged his followers to devote their lives to the cause, to fight God's battle to the end.

As soon as Judas Maccabeus took over the command, the little band of fighters, untrained and badly equipped as they were, began to gain real success in battle. Judas was a brave fighter and a brilliant general. He knew by instinct exactly when and where to fight, and how to deceive the enemy by making feints and false attacks. In the hour of battle he was like a lion in his fury and strength.

But Judas Maccabeus was not only a great soldier. He was a hero who showed in his own life all the fine qualities which heroic fighters so often lack. He never sought a battle for the sake of fighting; but fought only to rescue Jews who were being persecuted and oppressed, so that he might save their lives and restore to them their freedom to worship God. When the battle was over his fury left him, and he became the gentlest and kindest of men. He was admired for his courage and loved for his humanity; and so strong was his influence that his followers felt themselves inspired with something of their leader's strength and nobility, so that they too became heroes. Nor did Judas ever forget the cause for which he lived and fought. Before each battle he prayed to God for help, and resigned himself to the will of God in victory or defeat.

The rebel band under Judas Maccabeus gained their first victories in the highlands of Judea, and news of their successes brought many Jews out of hiding to join them. In their first pitched battle the Syrian commander was killed; and Judas, taking the dead man's sword, fought with it in every succeeding battle. A much larger force now pursued the Judeans to the mountains, determined to crush their resistance and wipe them out by force of arms and sheer weight of numbers. When the Judean warriors saw the Syrian army assembling near Beth-Horon they cried out in fear: "How can we wage war against such an enemy?" But Judas, by his own example of calm courage, stilled their fears; and reminded them of their duty to fight for the lives of their children and the Law of God. Then he led them in an attack of such energy and brilliance that the enemy was decisively beaten. Eight hundred Syrians lay dead on the field of battle: the remainder fled in panic westwards into the land of the Philistines.

Antiochus Epiphanes, seriously alarmed at the result of the battle of Beth-Horon, ordered one of his generals to open a new campaign. The Syrian general was so sure of victory that he invited slave traders to his camp, telling them to bring with them money and chains, as he had decided not to kill his Judean captives, but to sell them as slaves.

Meanwhile, Judas Maccabeus had assembled some 6,000 warriors in the mountain city of Mizpah. It was at Mizpah that 900 years earlier the prophet Samuel had assembled the people in order to choose a leader against the Philistines. And now, at Mizpah, Judas ordered a solemn day of fasting and prayer. With God, he told his soldiers, lay all hope of victory; and if they died fighting for their country, their laws and their religion, "you shall then obtain everlasting glory."

Judas Maccabeus divided his army into four divisions, placing three of them under the command of his brothers. With a final prayer: "As the will of God is in heaven, so let Him do," he led his forces down towards Emmaus in the plains, some eight or nine hours' march from Mizpah.

The Syrian general, when he learned that the Judeans were putting up their tents, resolved to attack the camp during the night. He reached it, to find no trace of the Judean army; and he decided that Judas Maccabeus had lost confidence and fled for safety to the mountains. He therefore divided his own forces, sending a division to pursue the Judeans and ordering the rest to return to camp. But Judas had not fled. At nightfall he had led his men by paths well known to him to the rear of the enemy encampment and had set fire to it. The Syrian army was thus divided; but it was not until daybreak that the Syrian general, who believed that he was hunting the Judeans to their mountain stronghold, turned to see that they had followed his army to the plains. Hurriedly he called a halt and ordered his division to return. In the meantime the Judeans had wiped out the rest of his army, and stood ready to engage the second division as it emerged from the mountains. But the battle was over. When the returning Syrians saw the smoke rising from their camp, they turned and fled in panic; and they left behind them large quantities of booty, including their helmets and shields and the sacks of money which the slave traders had brought at the command of the Syrian general.

The victory at Emmaus had been won by courage and strategy. It had shaken the power of the enemy and had filled the Judeans with confidence. They returned to their stronghold singing songs of joyful thanksgiving: "Praise the Lord, for He is good; for His mercy endureth for ever." And so, "Israel had a great deliverance that day."

This was not the end of the war. A year later the Syrian forces reformed and launched a fresh attack. There was a hotly fought battle at Beth-Zur, not far from Jerusalem; and once again victory went to the Judeans.

Then came the most exciting event of the whole campaign. In 165 B C E Judas Maccabeus and his followers marched into Jerusalem to free the city and to restore the Temple to the worship of God. The Temple was now a place of desolation; the doors had been burnt, the porches destroyed. Heathen images had been set up in the courts; and on the altar itself towered a statue of Zeus. Silently and swiftly Judas and his followers set about their work of cleansing the Temple. They removed the altar and pulled down and broke up the statues of the Greek gods. They made a new altar, erected new doors, and brought in fresh vessels and candlesticks. The whole work was completed in three weeks; and then the Temple was rededicated with thanksgiving and rejoicing.

For two thousand years Jews all over the world have commemorated the victories of Judas Maccabeus and the rededication of the Temple. The yearly festival is celebrated as the "Days of Consecration," or *Chanucah*. According to tradition, after the rededication the Temple lights burned for eight days, although there was only enough oil in the cruse for one day. And so, in remembrance, lights are kindled in Jewish homes and synagogues. One light is lit on the first night, two the second, and so on, until on the eighth and last night eight lights are burning, together with an extra—or "attendant"—light, which has been used to kindle the others. It is for this reason that the festival of *Chanucah* is also called the "Feast of Lights."

Even after the liberation of Jerusalem the war went on, for there still remained communities of Jews who had not yet been set free. Judas Maccabeus and his followers now pursued the enemy beyond the frontiers of Judea, into Galilee and Transjordan; and after each victorious raid the leader returned to Jerusalem, accompanied by Jews who rejoiced at their deliverance and who filled the Temple with songs of thanksgiving.

D

But the continuing good fortune of the Judeans caused the Syrian king to start war on an even larger scale. Antiochus Epiphanes, author of so much misery, had died soon after the rededication of the Temple, and his young son, Antiochus V, had succeeded him. The boy king accompanied his army on its march through Judea. It was a well-armed and a mighty force, and some of the officers were mounted on elephants. In order to defend Jerusalem and the Temple, Judas could spare only a small force to engage the enemy. He himself rode at the head of his troops, and encountered the Syrian army at Beth-Zachariah, not far from Beth-Zur. The Judeans fought as valiantly as ever, and without a thought for their own safety. Eleazor, one of Judas' brothers, died that day. He had, it is said, seen a splendidly dressed rider on one of the elephants, and, thinking that he must be the King, Eleazor had crept beneath the beast and stabbed it to death. But the rider was not the king; and Eleazor fell, crushed to death himself beneath the weight of the dying elephant.

Judas and the survivors of his army retired to Jerusalem to defend the Temple. The Syrians besieged the city, which was gallantly defended. But when supplies of food were exhausted, the Judeans began to desert, escaping by subterranean passages, until only Judas, his three surviving brothers, and a small, loyal band of their followers were left.

Yet, just when it seemed that the city must fall, the Syrian general received news that another enemy of Syria was marching on Antioch, the capital. In great haste he persuaded the young King to make peace with Judas. A treaty was signed which gave to the Judeans the right for which they had striven for so long—the right of all Jews to worship God in their own way. Then the Syrian army turned and rode away.

There was no real or lasting peace even now. It is very likely that, having gained religious freedom, Judas Maccabeus was seeking to make his country independent and to enlarge its borders. Then, too, the Greek way of life still had a powerful hold on some of the Judeans, who began to intrigue with the Syrians against Judas and his brothers. Once more—

in 160 B C E—Judas prepared to do battle. He sallied forth
with only a handful of loyal men to fling himself against the
enemy, who were encamped at Birat, near Bethlehem. The
little band of Judeans stood no chance; and their leader died
fighting, his sword still in his hand.

With the death of Judas there was renewed strife. But
twenty years later, when Rome had begun to dominate the
civilized world, Judea—under the Roman Empire—became
an independent province. And the High Priest and prince
of Judea was Simon, the wise statesman, the last of the sons
of Mattathias who had fought so long and so bravely for their
people and their faith. The name of Judas Maccabeus, the
greatest of them all, will never be forgotten. In the hearts of
his people he kindled lights as glowing as the lights he
kindled on the altar; and year by year his life is remembered
with thanksgiving.

HILLEL

(70 B C E - 10 CE)

"The humble, the pious"

THE rule of the descendants of the heroic Maccabees lasted for a hundred years; and then, after a family quarrel, civil war broke out. This led to intervention by Rome. The Roman general Pompey the Great, who had made a name for himself in his youth as a commander of men, captured Jerusalem. A terrible massacre of the Jews followed; and Judea, an independent province no longer, was forced into complete submission to all-powerful Rome.

Seven years before the fall of Jerusalem, in 70 B C E, a son had been born to a Jewish couple who lived in Babylon. According to tradition, the child was descended through his mother from the family of King David, and he was given the name of Hillel. Nothing is known of Hillel's childhood, not even the name of his father, although it is thought to have been Gamaliel. All that is known is that Hillel had a brother called Shebna. By the time the brothers had grown to manhood, the parents had become very poor. They must have been supported by their son Shebna, who was a merchant, for Hillel, who was a student and a scholar, was interested only in learning. It is said that Shebna suggested to Hillel that they should be partners. Hillel, who would be free to continue his studies, should share his knowledge with his brother, while Shebna, in return, would give Hillel a share

in the profits of his business. But Hillel, who loved only
learning and the Law, declined the offer and remained a
poor man.

When Hillel had learned all that the Babylonian schools
could teach him he journeyed to Jerusalem to study in a
greater school of learning. There the Law, with all its lesser
laws and regulations, was expounded by the leading teachers
of the day. Their names were Shemaiah and Abtalion, and
they were members of the Sanhedrin, the highest court of
justice and the supreme council of Jerusalem.

In the schools of learning of the day the teachers (or
rabbis as they later came to be called) not only taught and
expounded the Law, for which they received no payment,
but also followed a trade. The students did likewise, and
Hillel is thought to have been a woodcutter. He earned very
little; and out of his wages he now had to support a wife and
family with half his earnings and pay the other half as an
admission fee to the watchman of the school (or house of
study, as it was also called). One day, so the story goes,
Hillel had found no work at all, and the watchman (who was
entitled to keep the fee himself) would not admit him without
his usual payment. But so anxious was the young man not
to miss a word of the instruction, that he clambered up to a
skylight through which he could hear the lecture being given
in the room below. It was the eve of the Sabbath, a bitterly
cold winter's day; and during the night there was a snowfall,
a very rare occurrence in Jerusalem. Early next morning,
when the teachers entered the building, it was not only very
cold but very gloomy. "Brother Abtalion, our school is
strangely dark this morning," said Shemaiah. But when
they went to investigate they found that the darkness was
caused by the snow-covered figure of Hillel, who lay across
the skylight, half-frozen and quite unconscious. The teachers
hastened to pull him into the room; and although it was the
Sabbath and all work was forbidden, they kindled a fire,
prepared a hot bath, and rubbed Hillel's limbs with warm
oil. When he had revived they prepared a meal for him; and
as he ate they told one another that it was worth breaking

the Sabbath to help so earnest a scholar, who would keep many Sabbaths in return for the one they had broken.

At some time or other—we do not know when—Hillel left Jerusalem for a period of many years. Some people think that he went back to Babylon: others believe that he went to live in a community of pious Jews who spent their days in prayer, meditation and study. We next hear of him in Jerusalem about the year 30 BCE, when he was some forty years of age. By now Judea was under the rule of the man known as Herod the Great. Herod, whose family had been converted to Judaism, was appointed Governor of Judea in 47 BCE. He had no wish to make enemies of the Jews, but they feared him because of his friendship with Rome. Their fears were justified when seven years later Herod was made King of Judea; for he proved to be tyrannical and cruel. Like many of the Romans, Herod was a great builder. He restored ruined cities and fortifications, and, following the Roman example, he built theatres, arenas, circuses and baths in homage to the Roman Emperor. He also rebuilt the Temple, which had been plundered after Jerusalem fell to Pompey, and he rebuilt it with such magnificence that it became one of the wonders of the world.

Yet today, Herod is remembered only as a cruel tyrant, while the name of Hillel, the poor and humble scholar, is revered by Jews all over the world. The reason for this is not simply because Hillel, by the time he returned to Jerusalem, had become the foremost scholar of his day, but also because he had such a lovable personality. His love and trust in God was the first thing that people noticed; but second only to his love of God was his love of his fellow men and his faith in what they could achieve. He was generous, with a generosity which never made any man feel that he was accepting charity. He was humble, though not falsely humble; endlessly patient and endlessly kind. In any dispute he was on the side of peace and wise compromise; but perhaps his most outstanding quality was his extraordinary gentleness. In their efforts to keep the Jewish community together in the study of the Law (the *Torah* as we call it) and the worship of God, some of the Rabbis were narrow-minded and severe; but the gentle, peace-loving Hillel thought more of the spirit than the letter of the Law, and was as lenient as he could be in his interpretation.

So many stories are told about Hillel that it is not difficult to see him as he was. When he returned to Jerusalem, it is said, it was Passover time. That year the eve of the festival fell on the Sabbath. In each family it was the custom—in memory of the Passover in Egypt—for a lamb to be ceremonially killed as an offering to God, and later eaten by the family with unleavened bread and bitter herbs. The scholars were now debating whether, if they killed the lamb as usual, they would be breaking the Sabbath. They could not make up their minds; and then someone told them that a Babylonian, a pupil of the great Shemaiah and Abtalion, had arrived in the city, and suggested that he should be asked to decide. The Rabbis were rather amused, for they were inclined to despise the Jews who came from Babylon. All the same they agreed, and Hillel was brought in to answer the question. "Surely," he said, in reply, "there is not one Passover alone in the year that puts aside the Sabbath: there are many such." What he meant was that since charitable deeds and public offerings were made on every day of the week, the Sabbath included, there would be no harm in offering the lamb on the eve of this particular Passover.

The Rabbis, who did not understand what Hillel meant, scoffed at him as an ignorant Babylonian who thought there could be more than one Passover in the year. Even when he explained before the Sanhedrin that he meant no such thing the scholars refused to believe him until he told them that he was quoting the Law as it had been expounded by his teachers Shemaiah and Abtalion. Then, realizing that Hillel's knowledge of the Law was so much greater than their own, the members of the Sanhedrin appointed him as their head. But success did not make him proud; for he insisted that he owed his appointment not to his own learning but to the fact that he had been privileged—as others had not—to study under the famous teachers.

One of the things for which Hillel is best remembered is his "golden rule." The making of the rule happened in this way. There was in Jerusalem at the time another great teacher whose name was Shammai, who ranked second only to Hillel in the Sanhedrin. The two teachers often differed in their interpretation of the Law but the discussions between them and their students helped to clear many doubtful points. In character they were very different. While Hillel sought always to interpret the Law in a simple straightforward manner so that its observance could become a part of everyday life, Shammai was stern and severe in his interpretation. One day, it is said, a man went to Shammai and, sneering at the many rules and regulations of Judaism, challenged the Rabbi to teach him the whole of the Law while he stood on one foot. Shammai, in anger, told the man what he thought of him and sent him away. The man then went to Hillel and repeated his challenge. "What is hateful to you," said Hillel, "do not do to your fellow men. That is the whole *Torah*. The rest is explanation. Go, now and learn it." This short explanation, Hillel's "golden rule," shows the grandeur and the simplicity of Judaism. The rule was not a new one, for it had been expressed in the Book of Leviticus in the command: "Thou shalt love thy neighbour as thyself"; and it had always been part of the teaching of Judaism. But Hillel had shown that it was more than a part, for on a man's treatment of his fellow-men depended the whole of his religious life.

One of Hillel's many sayings which bear out the importance of his "golden rule" is: "Separate not thyself from the community." This means, of course, that it is wrong for any man to wrap himself up in his work or his family. He should live and work not only for himself and his family but for the good of all men. Hillel himself was a perfect example of the man who lived for the good of the community. Much as he loved to study, he was never too busy to talk with any one who came to him for advice or help; and he had a very special concern for the poor and the humbly born. Both Hillel and Shammai had a school of learning in Jerusalem.

Shammai chose students who were intelligent and modest, but he chose them from the homes of the well-born and the wealthy, because he thought they would make the best scholars. Hillel, on the other hand, took students from any home, rich or poor; for he believed that "one ought to teach every man." The poor, he thought, had just as much right to education as the rich. Today that idea is taken for granted but Hillel put it into practice nearly two thousand years ago.

In other ways, too, Hillel showed his care and concern for the poor, both to those who had always lived a life of hardship and to those who had met with misfortune. He never made gifts without first considering how best they could serve a man's needs. We are told that when once he learned that a wealthy man had lost all his possessions he gave the man a horse to ride on. And because it was the custom in wealthy families for a servant to run before a horseman to clear a path for him, he provided a servant as well as a horse.

The thoughtfulness which Hillel showed in his dealings with all men, his kindness and his patience were unshakable. In a lesser man, such humility might have caused a feeling of self-righteousness or priggishness. But Hillel possessed in addition a quiet and gentle sense of fun, which prevented him from taking himself too seriously. One day, we are told, two men who had heard many tales of Hillel's humility and patience, made a wager with one another. The wager was a large sum of money, and it would go to the man who first succeeded in making Hillel angry. One of the two, choosing the most inconvenient time he could, called at Hillel's house shortly before the Sabbath came in at intervals of a few minutes. Each time he asked the master a pointless question, to which Hillel replied with patience and perfect good temper. In the end, realizing that Hillel's patience really was inexhaustible, the man demanded in a very insulting voice: "Are you the Hillel whom they call the prince of Israel?" Now Hillel had been given the title of *nasi*, which means prince, or president, of the Sanhedrin; and so he replied that he was indeed called prince. "Well," said the man

rudely, "I hope there are not many like you in Israel."
"Why not, my son?" asked Hillel. "Because through you,"
said the man, "I have just lost a large sum of money."
"Then, take care," said Hillel with a smile, "I may cause
you to lose much money but I will not easily lose my
patience." And he went on to tell the man that the money
was not entirely wasted if its loss prevented him from making
foolish wagers in future.

Sometimes Hillel would tease or puzzle his students with
his remarks. One day, when one of them asked where he
was going, he replied: "To do a pious deed." "What may
that be?" the student enquired. "To take a bath," replied
his master. Mystified, the student asked: "Is that a pious
deed?" "Yes," answered Hillel. And he went on to explain
that if the images of the Roman Emperor which his Roman
subjects had set up in the theatres and circuses were regularly cleaned, how much more important was it for man to
care for his body, since man had been created in the image
of God.

Another day Hillel told his students that he must leave
them and hurry home to the guest in his house. When they
asked if there was always a guest in his house, he answered:
"Is not my poor soul a guest in the body? Today it is here,
tomorrow it is gone."

In history there have been many wise men who thought
that it was good for their souls to starve their bodies. But
Hillel, so much wiser than they, knew that a bath and food
helped to give a man the clear brain and the energy which he
needed for long periods of study.

The results of Hillel's study are very important indeed.
His chief work was to put in order the traditional Law. This
had been handed down by scholars from generation to generation and through the years many rules and regulations had
been added to it. Some of these minor laws were so complicated that it was hard to understand what they meant. But
Hillel's knowledge was so wide and so deep that he was able
to frame rules which explained the minor laws; and, as we
have seen, he never made them unreasonably strict but

sought always to keep them in line with everyday life. Hillel
did not live to complete the task, which was taken up after
his death by other great scholars. But we owe to Hillel a
beginning in the work of compiling the Code of Laws (or
Mishnah, as it is called) and many decisions on doubtful
points.

A single example will show something of what he achieved.
There was in existence a law, which took effect every
seventh year, that if a man borrowed money from another
and could not repay the loan, the man who had lent the
money had to make his debtor a present of it. This law had
been described in the Book of Deuteronomy: "At the end of
every seven years thou shalt make a release. And this is the
manner of the release: Every creditor that lendeth ought
unto his neighbour shall release it; he shall not exact it of
his neighbour, or of his brother; because it is the Lord's
release."

The law had originally been made to protect the poor
against the rich; and it had been made at a time when money
did not change hands and a loan would be made up of corn,
fruit or goats. By Hillel's day, when loans were often of
money, the law was pressing hardly on rich and poor alike.
As the seventh year approached, a rich man would refuse
to lend to a poor man knowing, as he did, that the loan
would probably never be repaid. The rich man would
therefore lose the interest his money might have earned; the
poor man would not receive his loan. Realizing this hardship,
Hillel arranged for the lender (or creditor) to transfer his
claim from the man to whom he had lent money to the
judges who served on the Council of Elders. In this way—
as the law required—the rich man gave up his debt; but he
could, if he wished, recover his money. When he transferred
the debt to the judges the money was no longer considered
to be owing to him. Instead, it was considered to be owing to
the Council of Elders; and it was a matter of self-respect
(as well as a law) for a debt to the Council to be repaid as
soon as possible. And so, in every seventh year, rich men
continued to make loans, which they could recover by applying

to the Council. This arrangement, which was called a *prosbul*, proved equally helpful to creditor and debtor.

And so, teaching and building up the *Mishnah*, Hillel grew to old age, still striving for peace and forbearance among all men, still making wise and kindly decisions on points of law. It is told that an argument once arose between the students of the two schools of Hillel and Shammai as to how the *Shema* should be recited. Shammai's students, who tended to be even more strict and severe than their master, insisted that in the evening it should be said lying down and in the morning standing up, so that the words of the command should be fulfilled: "And thou shalt talk of them . . . when you liest down, and when thou risest up." But Hillel's students maintained that it did not matter how or where the *Shema* was recited. A bricklayer might pause in his work, a fruit-picker in a tree might put down his basket to say: "Hear, O Israel! The Lord our God, the Lord is One!" All that mattered was that the words should be said and their meaning understood.

It is not surprising that the gentle Hillel was loved above all other teachers. When his students realized that he was going to die, they entered his room one by one to ask his blessing—all save one, Johanan ben Zakkai, who had humbly remained outside. When the old master had blessed his students and said farewell to them he asked: "Where is he, the youngest among you, he who is destined to be the father of wisdom and the father of generations to come?" Johanan ben Zakkai was brought into the room; and when Hillel saw the young man he quoted the words used in the Book of Proverbs to describe Wisdom: "I will endow with substance those who love me and fill their treasuries."

And so Hillel died. He was mourned throughout the whole country, and people spoke of him as "the humble, the pious, the disciple of Ezra"; for, like Ezra, the great priest and scribe, Hillel had come to Jerusalem from Babylon. As a mark of their affection they arranged for the office of president of the Sanhedrin to be held always by one of Hillel's descendants. Of Hillel's son, Simon I, who succeeded him as president, nothing is known but his name. But Hillel had bequeathed to his students something of his own greatness and gentleness. Throughout many troubled years the School of Hillel was to remain like an island of peace and wisdom set in a stormy sea.

AKIBA
(53 CE-135)
Teacher, Scholar and Martyr

ALTHOUGH outwardly the Jews had submitted completely to Roman rule, they dreamed of freedom. But among themselves they were not united; and when the more hot-headed among them—the Zealots, as they were called—planned to break free by violent means, the more law-abiding people were greatly troubled.

The gentle Hillel had been right when he spoke on his death-bed of his youngest student, Johanan ben Zakkai, as a man destined to be the father of wisdom and the father of generations to come. Johanan became a member of the Sanhedrin and a teacher who, like Hillel, sought always the peaceful way. He knew only too well that if the Jews rebelled they must in the end be crushed by the power of Rome, and he did his utmost to prevent a revolt. He failed; and the Zealots headed a Jewish rebellion.

Then Johanan made up his mind that, come what may, the religion and the Law of his people should be preserved, even if the Temple were destroyed, as he feared it would be. The Roman army had gathered outside Jerusalem and was battering at the walls as Johanan pondered how best to carry out his resolution. The Zealots called him a traitor because he had attempted to prevent the rebellion; and if he had asked for permission to leave the city it would have been refused.

One evening, it is said, a coffin was carried to the city gates. The sentinels had been given orders that no one should pass; and when the bearers told them that the coffin contained the body of Johanan ben Zakkai, who had recently died, they threatened to run it through with their swords. The coffin-bearers cried out in horror at such disrespect to the dead, and so the sentinels let them pass.

Safely beyond the city walls they set down their burden and opened the coffin to release Johanan, who had only been feigning death. Johanan hurried to the camp of the Roman general, to present a petition. When the general learned that Johanan had been one of those who advocated peace, he agreed to the Rabbi's modest request that he should be allowed to settle in the little town of Jamnia on the Mediterranean coast and there continue his work of teaching.

Then the Roman legions advanced against Jerusalem; and in the year 70 of the Common Era the defenders surrendered. The Romans sacked the city and burned the Temple to ashes. They massacred thousands of Jews, sold thousands more into slavery or drove them into banishment. And so the Jewish state was brought to a violent end.

Jerusalem was now like a city of the dead: but the *Torah* had been saved. At Jamnia Johanan ben Zakkai had founded a school of learning in which the study of the Law had never ceased. So now, to Jamnia flocked the students who were to preserve the Law for their descendants, and keep alight the living faith of Judaism.

In time, students from Jamnia who were called *Tannaim* (meaning "teachers") went out to found other schools of learning in the country, which was now known as Palestine. It was more necessary than ever before for Jews to whom Judaism was the One Religion to keep strong in their faith. Many Jews, especially those who lived in Galilee in the north of Palestine, were accepting other teaching. By the time the Temple was destroyed, Jesus of Nazareth (Nazareth was a city of Galilee) had lived and preached, and had been crucified by the Romans. Jesus was a profound student of Jewish Law. Much of his teaching resembled the teaching of Hillel; for Jesus taught, as Hillel had taught, the virtues of humility, gentleness and peace.

After the death of Jesus his followers spread his teaching; for they saw in him the chosen deliverer of the Jews, and believed that his coming had been foretold in the Old Testament. They called Jesus the Christ and the Messiah (which also means "deliverer"); and they gained many adherents among the Jews and among the pagans. And so began a new religion, the religion of Christianity. It started with a mere handful of converts; but it is a faith which has inspired vast numbers of people all over the world.

Christianity contains much of Jewish Law and teaching: but the central idea of Jesus as the Christ, the divine ruler of men, the Son of God, is one which no believing Jew could accept. And so down the ages, despite trials such as no other religious people has had to endure, the Jews have clung to their Judaism.

When the followers of Jesus first began to spread his teaching—about the year 50 of the Common Era—a boy was born of humble Jewish parents. His name was Akiba ben Joseph (Akiba, son of Joseph), and he was brought up to be a shepherd. We are told that the boy's master was a wealthy citizen of Jerusalem named Joshua. Joshua, a proud and arrogant man, was horrified to learn that his beautiful daughter Rachel and this ignorant young shepherd were in love with one another and planning to marry. He refused to give his consent to the marriage; and when Rachel persisted, he disinherited her and swore that he would never see her again.

Rachel cared nothing about money. All she wanted was that Akiba, a very intelligent young man, should be given an opportunity to study. When they married the young couple were extremely poor, for naturally Akiba could no longer work for her father. Somehow they found enough money to keep them while Akiba attended lectures, but often they did not have enough to eat. So poor were they, the story goes, that Rachel cut off her beautiful hair and sold it to help her husband. Yet, despite their poverty, they were extremely

generous. Once, when their only bed was a bundle of straw,
a man came to their home to beg for some straw to make a
bed for his wife who was ill. Akiba at once divided the
bundle and gave half to the man, remarking to Rachel that,
poor as they might be, there were others still poorer.

When Akiba had learned all he could in his home village
not far from Jerusalem, Rachel persuaded him to go away to
study in one of the famous schools of learning. Her faith in
him was justified, for he became a wise and profound
scholar, so far ahead of his fellows that before many years
had passed he had been appointed head of the school, and
reports of his learning spread far and wide.

At last the time came for him to return to his own village.
He set out on his journey accompanied by a crowd of
followers, each one a scholar in his own right. The arrival
of a famous Rabbi in a small village was a great event and
the whole population gathered to welcome him. Among them
was a shabbily dressed woman, haggard and thin and old
before her time. When she tried to reach Akiba's side some
of his followers barred the way. But Akiba had recognized
the thin, tired woman as his beloved wife Rachel, and he
pushed through the crowd to take her in his arms. "For
what I am," he told his followers, "and for what you are, to
this noble woman the thanks are due." Humbled by the
knowledge that for the sake of learning Rachel had patiently
endured hardship and want for so many years, Akiba's
followers crept silently away, leaving husband and wife
together.

Not long after this, Rachel's father Joshua, ignorant of the
famous Rabbi's identity, came to ask his advice. Evidently
his conscience had been troubling him, for he wanted to
know if it were possible for him to break a vow. His only
daughter, he told the Rabbi, had insisted on marrying an
ignorant beggar, and he had vowed never to forgive her or
see her again. But now, in his old age, he longed to see her
and share his wealth with her. Could he, in honesty, go back
on his word?

"Was it because the man was ignorant," asked Akiba

E

with a smile, "or was it because he was poor? Would you have refused to forgive your daughter if she had married a scholar?"

Amazed at such a question, Joshua replied that he would have been delighted for his daughter to marry a scholar. He would have welcomed the least brilliant of the Rabbi's students as a son-in-law.

"Well, then," said the Rabbi, "I know not if I am the scholar that men call me, but I certainly am the Akiba who married your daughter."

Joshua was filled with remorse when he realized what his daughter had suffered. But Rachel and Akiba bore him no malice. Now Akiba and his devoted wife and their children could live in comfort instead of poverty. Prestige had not changed Akiba, and wealth did not change him either. He had always been a modest man, and he looked on wealth only as a means of helping other people. One of his often-repeated sayings shows what importance he placed on the value of modesty: "Take thy place a few seats below thy rank until thou art bidden to take a higher place; for it is better that they should say to thee 'Come up higher' than that they should bid thee 'Go down lower'." He often warned his students not to be conceited about their learning; never to be so sure of themselves that they tried to interpret the Law without thinking over very carefully beforehand what they intended to say.

The study of the Law was always Akiba's deepest interest, and, like Hillel before him, love of study was bound up with faith in God. Once a man came to him and asked him who had created the world. Akiba replied that God had created it. The man demanded a positive proof. Akiba countered with a question of his own. He asked the man who had woven the cloth for the clothes he was wearing. "A weaver," answered the man. "I do not believe you," said Akiba. "Give me a positive proof." Annoyed, the man replied that proof was not necessary, for every one knew that a weaver must have made the cloth. "Even so," replied the Rabbi, "you must know that God created the world." When the man had gone Akiba explained to his students that just as there would be no cloth without a weaver, no house without a builder, there would be no world if God had not created it. Life, he also told them, was a loan made to man by God. It was for man to make the best use he could of the loan before he died and rendered account of it.

Faith did not mean to Akiba, as it meant to some people, that a man should treat all misfortunes as though they were the will of God. He believed—as Hillel believed—that man had a duty to his body as well as to his mind and soul. One day he was walking with another scholar in the streets of Jerusalem, when a man approached them, told them he was ill and asked their advice. The Rabbis told him of a remedy; but, instead of being pleased, the man reproached them for their lack of faith. Surely, he said, it was God's will that a man should fall ill; and it would be acting against the will of God for another man to prescribe a remedy and effect a cure. "What is your occupation?" the Rabbis enquired. The man replied that he was a gardener. If he believed what he had just told them, said Rabbi Akiba, why did he not leave the care of the earth to God who had created it? But, the man objected, if he did not manure and water the ground and prune the trees they would bear no fruit. "Man," was the answer, "is like the trees of the field." He must work to protect the loan of life which God had made him.

Akiba resembled Hillel in his thoughtful kindness. Once, we learn, he went to see one of his students who was ill. He found the young man quite alone, and stayed with him until he was better, nursing and feeding him, and even cleaning the room and scrubbing the floor. "Rabbi," said the grateful student, "you have given me a new life." Afterwards Akiba would often speak of man's duty to help the sick. "He who does not visit a sick person," he said, "is as if he shortens his life."

Akiba's special contribution to the study of the Law was the explanation of some of the rules and regulations, a continuation of the work which Hillel had begun. He was also famed for his great work on the Old Testament. With other scholars he gave long and careful thought to the books which should be included in the Bible and those which should be rejected. And in order that those Jews who understood only Greek should be able to read the Old Testament, he arranged for a special translation to be made into Greek.

There was one way in which Akiba and Hillel differed very strongly. Hillel, and after him Johanan ben Zakki, had striven always to keep the peace: but Akiba, who was a sterner man, became involved in a struggle which proved disastrous.

Ever since the destruction of the Temple there were Jews who dreamed of freedom; and once again—in the year 132— they rebelled against Rome. Their leader was a brave and splendid young soldier; and people began to believe that he was not simply a daring leader, but was, in fact, the Messiah, who had come at last to deliver the Jews and restore the kingdom of Israel. People recalled the saying from the Book of Numbers: "There shall come a star out of Jacob who shall smite the corners of Moab and destroy all the children of Seth." And so they called their leader Bar Cochba, which means "Son of a Star." Even Rabbi Akiba, wise and learned as he was, believed that Bar Cochba was the appointed deliverer; and because Akiba was so much loved and respected, many people followed his example and believed as he did.

Half a million men flocked to Bar Cochba's standard, some of them recruited by Akiba, who went about the country seeking help. At first all went well. Like Judas Maccabeus before him, Bar Cochba had an amazing series of victories. He repulsed the Roman Legions, captured fortress after fortress; and finally, in triumph, he entered ruined Jerusalem, which the Roman Emperor was determined to rebuild as a pagan city.

The Roman Emperor, Hadrian, who had imagined at first that the situation would be easy to handle, now became seriously alarmed. He therefore set his most successful general at the head of his army with orders to put down the rebellion at any cost. With the new appointment the tide turned against the Jews. One by one the fortresses they had captured fell to the Romans, until only Bethar, the strongest, remained. Bar Cochba held out at Bethar for a whole year. Again and again at the head of his troops he sallied out and tried to cut his way through the Roman forces; but each time he had to retire after inflicting heavy casualties on the enemy. In the end, after starvation and sickness among the defenders had caused fearful losses, a treacherous informer led the Romans into the stronghold by a secret way. In the fight which followed many of the Romans were slain; and the slaughter of the defenders which followed their defeat was more terrible than any that had occurred before. Bar Cochba, derided as a false Messiah by the very people who had once acclaimed him, did not survive the fall of Bethar.

The Emperor Hadrian was now determined to stamp out Judaism once and for all, so that never again would there be people foolhardy enough to defend it. He ordered a plough-share to be passed over the ruins of Jerusalem, and the foundations of a pagan city were laid. He also issued an edict that no one was to study the Law on pain of death. Rabbi Akiba, whose support of Bar Cochba was known to the Romans, refused absolutely to obey the edict and continued his studies as though it had never been issued.

One day a friend, terrified of what might happen to Akiba, came to him and begged him to submit. "Let me tell you a story," the Rabbi said. "A fox, walking along the banks of a river, looked down in pity at the fish struggling in the water. 'Why are you so frightened?' he asked. 'Some men are spreading their nets to catch us,' replied the fish, 'and we are trying to escape.' 'Then come on land,' advised the fox, 'and we will live together in peace and safety.' 'Are you indeed the fox,' exclaimed the fish, 'who is considered the wisest of animals? You are certainly the most stupid if you give us such advice. The water is our native element, and if we are in danger in the river, we should be in far greater danger on land'." And it was the same with the Jews, Akiba concluded. "Our element is the Law. If we forsake it, we destroy ourselves."

Akiba's friend, realizing that nothing would change him, went sadly away. A short time after the Rabbi was arrested by the Romans and condemned to die by torture. Akiba faced death with unflinching courage. In the midst of his sufferings he realized that it was time for morning prayers, and in a clear, firm voice he recited the *Shema*: "Hear, O Israel! The Lord our God, the Lord is One." Overcome by the bravery of the dying man the executioner asked him if he had felt no pain. "I feel the pain," replied Akiba, "but I have often promised in prayer to love my God with all my heart, with all my soul, and with all my might. This means even if I lose my life. Now that my life is demanded of me, should I not rejoice that I am able to hallow the name of God aloud?" And so saying, the heroic Rabbi died.

The Romans, who had destroyed Akiba's body, had not destroyed the Law nor put an end to his influence. The Jews who grieved at Akiba's death treasured his wise sayings. And from his school of learning there came many other scholars to keep alive the spirit of their faith.

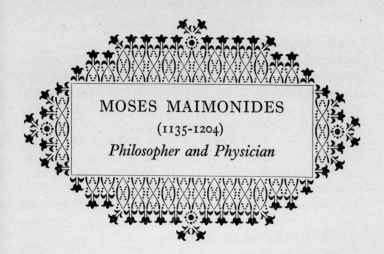

MOSES MAIMONIDES
(1135-1204)
Philosopher and Physician

Aᴌᴛʜᴏᴜɢʜ the Roman Emperors who came after Hadrian lifted some of the harsh laws he had imposed, most of the Jews who had survived the suppression of Bar Cochba's revolt fled from Judea to settle in the northern part of Palestine or to go farther afield in search of freedom and peace.

For a time the scholars remained, quietly continuing their work of collecting and explaining a vast mass of laws and of the literature which had evolved from the laws. The whole collection is known as the *Talmud*, which means "lesson." The *Talmud* is made up of two parts, the *Mishneh* and the *Gemara*. The *Mishneh*, which means "learning," is the Oral (or spoken) Law: it had been handed down and added to from generation to generation until Hillel began the work of putting it in order. The work, which went on after Hillel's death, was finished in about 200 ᴄ ᴇ by another great scholar, Rabbi Judah ha Nasi (Judah "the Prince"), who, according to tradition, was born on the day of Rabbi Akiba's tragic death. The *Mishneh* provided a guide, an authority to which Jews could refer. But often when they consulted the *Mishneh* they found that the rules which it laid down were not clear enough for them to understand; and so the *Gemara*, which means "completion," was added. The *Gemara* is an explanation and an interpretation of the *Mishneh*. The *Talmud* in its completed form—composed of *Mishneh* and *Gemara*—contains laws, history, stories, prayers and meditations, together with many discussions on religious subjects.

In actual fact, two versions of the *Talmud* were being prepared. The first—the Palestine *Talmud*—was left unfinished. The second was compiled in Babylon. Ever since the exile which followed the Babylonian conquest of Judah there had been a settlement of Jews in Babylon, and it had grown through the years. Babylon, which like Palestine had schools of Jewish learning, soon became the core of Jewish life; and in the Babylonian schools work continued on the *Talmud* until about the year 500. The Babylonian *Talmud* is the version most generally studied today. It is one of the great books of the world; and, next to the Bible, it has had the strongest influence on the Jewish way of life through the centuries.

In Babylon, under Persian rule, the Jews were free and equal citizens with the Babylonians, with the same duties and privileges. A very different state of affairs prevailed in Palestine. Since the Bar Cochba revolt Jews had been forbidden to enter Jerusalem, although Christians—who had taken no part in the revolt—were allowed to go in and out of the new Roman city as they wished.

When Christianity replaced the worship of many gods as the official religion of the Roman Empire—and this did not happen until many Christians had faced martyrdom rather that abandon their faith—fresh restrictions were placed on the Jews. For this reason more and more of them left their homes to join the groups of Jews who had already settled in Egypt, in Arabia beyond the borders of Babylon, in Asia and on the island of Cyprus in the Mediterranean. In due course they reached Europe. The first European Jews were prisoners captured by the Romans and sold as slaves to European owners. Later, Jewish traders and merchants began to visit Europe, and by the beginning of the fourth century there were Jewish settlements in Greece, Italy, Spain and in what is now Germany.

Until the beginning of the seventh century Babylon remained the centre of Jewish life and learning; but then an event occurred which put a violent end to peace and freedom. A new religion had been born—Islam. Islam was founded by Mohammed, who was born in the year 570, in Mecca in Arabia. Mohammed proclaimed his belief in one god—Allah—and declared himself to be the prophet of Allah. By his constant preaching he gathered around him a small but fiercely devoted band of followers, known as Moslems; and he then began an amazing series of conquests. Babylon was seized from its Persian rulers, Palestine and the whole of Arabia were overrun. The conquerors gave their victims the choice of death or conversion to Islam; and in this way they made many converts. The *Koran*, the Sacred Book of Islam, had something in it of Jewish Law: but the Jews, loyal to their own faith, refused to accept Islam, and many of them were slain or driven out of Arabia. Mohammed died in 632. By that time Islam was firmly established; and although "unbelievers" were not everywhere given the terrible choice of death or conversion, it remained a power to be feared. When finally the persecution of "unbelievers" ceased, Islam could be seen as the third of the great religions of the world. Judaism was the first; Christianity the second; and Islam, like Christianity, had sprung from Judaism.

With the conquest of Palestine, Babylon and Arabia another centre of Jewish life arose, this time in Europe. In 711 a band of Arabs (or Moors as they were generally called) crossed the Straits of Gibraltar from North-west Africa and conquered Spain. The Moors were Moslems; but in many ways they resembled the Jews, whom they respected and encouraged to settle in Spain. For four hundred years Spain remained a refuge. Elsewhere Jews existed only on sufferance, hedged in by troublesome laws and prohibitions which all too often led to oppression and persecution. But in Spain —as once in Babylon—the Jews were safe and free to observe their religion. A Jew who had proved his worth could gain high office in the government; and many Jews distinguished themselves in the service of the state, while others made their name as scholars, writers, scientists and philosophers.

Towards the end of the twelfth century, however, another band of Moslems from North Africa (known as the Almohades) invaded Spain and conquered the southern part of the country. Unlike the kindly Moors, they were fiercely opposed to any religion except their own. "No church and no synagogue" was their war-cry; and to Christians and Jews alike they gave the choice of conversion, exile or death. The choice was not a very difficult one for the Christians: northern Spain was a Christian country and there they found a welcome and a home. But there was no welcome for the Jews, either in northern Spain or anywhere else. In desperation, some Jews agreed to accept the teachings of Islam. They attended services in the mosques and in public kept its observances. But in their hearts they were still Jews, and they preserved their own faith in secret. The great majority of the Jews rejected this compromise. They refused to pay lip-service to Islam, and so they chose exile, wandering from place to place in a hopeless quest for a home.

A short time before this—on the Eve of Passover, 1135— a Jewish boy was born in the city of Cordova in Andalusia, part of southern Spain. The boy's father was named Maimon, and the child was given the name of Moses ben Maimon, Moses the son of Maimon. Later in life he became known, not as Moses ben Maimon but as Moses Maimonides—the Greek version of his name; and that is the name by which he is remembered today.

Maimon was a very learned man, a member of the rabbinical college of Cordova; and his family had lived in Andalusia for generations. Like other Spanish Jewish scholars, he had studied scientific subjects and he had written books on mathematics and astronomy as well as on subjects connected with the *Talmud*. With his father the boy Moses studied the Bible and the *Talmud* and a certain amount of science; and he also began to study medicine and philosophy—the search for the nature and meaning of truth and human knowledge.

Moses ben Maimon was thirteen when Cordova was captured by the fanatical Almohades. His father bravely refused to accept Islam, knowing that this meant exile. But although Maimon would not, even in public, pay service to another religion, he decided that it would give his family some measure of protection if, on their wanderings, they wore the Arab turban and robe. The family spoke Arabic fluently; but, even so, they were in constant danger of being discovered as Jews. For safety's sake they journeyed from city to city, staying only a short time in each.

Although the churches and synagogues of southern Spain had been destroyed, a few schools of learning still existed; and so, from time to time, Moses and his younger brother David enjoyed a few weeks or months of study. David, who was not a scholar, grew up to be a trader in trinkets and precious stones; while Moses, who had shown signs of brilliance as a boy, soon eclipsed his father. The family could not take many books with them on their travels; but Moses, who had a wonderful memory, never forgot anything he had learned.

For about ten years Maimon, with his two sons and a daughter, wandered restlessly about Spain. Then, in despair, they left the country of their birth and sailed across the Mediterranean to Morocco in North Africa. Life was not quite so dangerous in North Africa at the time, and they found a temporary home in Fez, where they lived for five years. There, Moses buried himself in his studies, while David, the younger brother, generously became the support of the whole family.

Before very long news came to Fez of the plight of those Jews who had made a pretence of accepting Islam. Worn down by fear and constant danger, they felt they could no longer observe their Judaism even in secret and were planning to abandon it altogether. To encourage the waverers to remain loyal to their faith, Maimon composed a letter known as the *Letter of Consolation*; and he wrote it in Arabic, a language which all the Jews of the East understood. In it he urged the Jews never to despair or to imagine that

God had forgotten them. The Law of God, he said, was like a strong cord suspended from earth to heaven. A man who took a firm hold of the cord "with his whole hand has, doubtless, more hope than he who clings to it with but part of it, but he who clings on with the tips of his fingers has more hope than he who lets go of it altogether."

The assurance that it was better to cling to the cord with fingertips only (which was another way of advising the Jews who dared not reveal their faith openly to cling to it in secret) gave fresh hope to the waverers. But, meanwhile, a Moroccan Jew had written to a rabbi who lived far away from the scene of persecution to know if it was permitted for a Jew to pay lip-service to Islam in order to save his life. The rabbi, who was himself in no danger, replied that a Jew who made the declaration which the Moslems demanded —"there is no God but Allah, and Mohammed is his prophet"—was no better than an idolater. This ruling brought despair to those who had made the declaration, but who had continued to consider themselves Jews. And their despair was the deeper when they understood that they were being called on to make a public confession; for they knew only too well that the punishment for a convert to Islam who reverted to his former religion was death.

Maimon and his son Moses realized at once that while some of the terrified Jews would renounce Islam and courageously face a martyr's death, those whose faith was weak would give up their religion in order to save their lives. Moses was by now a young man of twenty-five, earnest, serious and sympathetic. It was all-important to him to preserve Judaism as a living faith. Jews were in a minority everywhere, living in perilous conditions; and if thousands of them allowed themselves to be killed and thousands more abandoned their religion, there would be a grave danger of Judaism dying out. He therefore set to work to write an essay—a *Letter on Conversion*. In it he said that if a Jew deliberately chose martyrdom he "had done nobly and well, and his reward is great before the Lord." Then he went on to write comforting words to the waverers. "But if any man

asks me: 'Shall I be slain or utter the formula of Islam?'
I answer, 'Utter the formula and live.' "

The *Letter* had the effect of drawing thousands of
frightened Jews back to their faith. Henceforward they
looked on Moses ben Maimon as a true friend and as an
adviser on the Jewish way of life; and, for his part, Moses
was only too eager to help. But by now the Mohammedan
authorities had become suspicious, and a Moslem friend
came secretly to see Moses and to warn him that he was
about to be arrested. Moses decided that he and his family
must leave Fez at once.

So once again the family of Maimon was homeless. They
dared not attempt to leave the country by day for fear of
being caught and brought back; but they managed to escape
under cover of darkness, made their way to the coast and
boarded a ship which was sailing for Palestine.

The journey took a month. It started well enough, but on
the seventh day there was a violent storm and the little ship
almost foundered in the high seas. At length the storm died
down; and Moses made a solemn vow to observe the first
and seventh days of the voyage every year with prayers and
fasting. The first day commemorated the family's escape
from death by persecution; the seventh their escape from
death by drowning.

Palestine, although still influenced by Islam, was at this
time under Christian rule. A few Jewish families lived there,
scattered all over the country, and they made the Maimon
family welcome. But Palestine was no longer a land of
Jewish learning; the Jews, though kind, were ignorant; and
Moses, who longed for the companionship of scholars,
decided not to settle there. After a short stay the family left
for Egypt; and in 1165 they found a permanent home at
Fostat, near Cairo.

In Egypt they discovered that the Jews had been given the
right to observe their religion; and before long they were
granted other privileges, including freedom to manage their
own affairs under a Jewish Nagid (or Prince). Egypt was soon
to come under the rule of a new Sultan. He was Saladin, a

great champion of Islam, but a foe to Christianity. Saladin was the enemy against whom Richard I of England was to lead an army in the Third Crusade, which lasted from 1189 to 1192. These Crusades were expeditions carried out by some of the Christian nations of Europe against the Moslems in Palestine. Their object was to ensure the safety of pilgrims to the Holy Places of Christendom and to keep the Holy Places in Christian hands.

Saladin, three years younger than Moses ben Maimon (or Maimonides as he should now be called), became the supreme ruler of Egypt in 1174, and was a good friend and patron of his Jewish subjects. When the Maimon family settled at Fostat they must have thought that their troubles were over; but almost at once the gentle, scholarly Maimon died, worn out by the years of anxiety and wandering.

A few years later Moses had to face another loss. David, his merchant brother, had gone on a sea voyage across the Indian Ocean on his way to buy fresh stocks of precious stones, taking with him for the purchase a large sum of money lent to him by Moses and a number of friends. He never returned; and later on news reached Fostat that the ship had foundered and every soul on board had been lost.

Moses Maimonides was overcome with grief at the death of his younger brother. His own health had been ruined just as his father's had been, and now for months he lay sick, "afflicted," as he wrote, "with fever and despair." But, ill as he was, he had to rouse himself to take on the responsibility of supporting David's widow and little girl as well as his own wife and children, for he himself had married soon after he arrived in Egypt. He had never had to think about earning a living before, since David's generosity had kept the whole family in comfort. He might have used his knowledge of the Bible and the *Talmud* to gain a livelihood; but the day had not yet come when a rabbi would accept payment for his work. So Moses decided to become a physician. He had always been extremely interested in medicine and had studied it from boyhood onwards. As he was quite unknown as a doctor he had very few patients to begin with and he charged very low fees. In order to earn enough to keep the family he also gave lectures on philosophy.

Moses was the kind of man who does everything he undertakes extremely well. He loved study; but he was not the sort of scholar who loves learning only for its own sake. What he learned he wanted to impart to others, and because he could explain and simplify the most difficult subjects he was an ideal teacher. Before he began his career as a physician he was known for his writings on Jewish questions. Very early in life he had come to the conclusion that the ordinary Jew could not give nearly enough time to the study of the *Talmud*. It was true that in the *Talmud* he had a guide; but in spite of the work which had been put into compiling it, the *Talmud* could be understood only by the most scholarly Jews; and even they were confused by discussions which led to no decision. To most Jews, the *Mishneh* was vague and puzzling and the *Gemara* did not really explain it. Moses Maimonides had therefore written his own commentary on the *Mishneh*. In it he cut away a great deal of information and discussion which no longer seemed to apply to Jewish life: and he explained, clearly and correctly, many vague and obscure passages, sometimes using an explanation from the *Talmud*, sometimes taking it from the writings of more recent scholars. In fact, he produced what today we would call a "popular" guide to a complicated subject.

Besides his *Commentary on the Mishneh*, Moses Maimonides wrote two other big and very important works, the *Mishneh Torah*, and the *Guide to the Perplexed*. The *Mishneh Torah* (or Repetition of the *Torah*), which he completed when he was forty-five, was a rearrangement of the Law in such a form that it was easy to consult. He knew that the laws contained in the Bible and the *Talmud*, as well as the commentaries which had been made on them, had not been placed in good order; and this meant that the average Jew—and sometimes even the scholar—who wanted to make sure that something he planned to do was not forbidden by Jewish Law would often lose himself completely in his search for an answer to his question. Moses Maimonides therefore collected all the laws and commentaries together and arranged them in fourteen different books. In one book, for example, he placed all the laws and commentaries concerned with agriculture; in another those concerning ceremonial; in two more those concerned with crime. But the *Mishneh Torah* was something more than a repetition of the Law in a handy form. It showed clearly the justice and mercy of Jewish Law and it proved that Judaism is a religion which demands from man the highest spiritual qualities.

With the appearance of his *Mishneh Torah*, Moses Maimonides became the most famous authority in the Jewish world. Although it received a great deal of praise, however, some people disapproved of it strongly. They were afraid that it would prevent scholars from consulting the *Talmud* itself; and they also feared that its immense popularity would make the author conceited and arrogant. They need not have been afraid. Scholars continued to refer their problems to the *Talmud* while other men consulted the *Mishneh Torah;* and Moses Maimonides remained quite unspoilt and as eager as ever to help the ordinary man.

For this reason he started another book, which he called his *Guide to the Perplexed*. His object was to explain to puzzled but religious people how the teachings of philosophy harmonized with the teachings of religion. Many people imagined that philosophy—the search for truth and knowledge—would destroy the idea of a God of religion. But, argued Moses Maimonides, both religion and philosophy recognize the existence of a single Creator. The God of religion is therefore also the God of truth; and so religion and philosophy can be united in the worship of God.

The *Guide* showed that Moses Maimonides had other very progressive ideas. The Word of God, he said, was intended for all people; but this did not mean that every single passage in the Bible was meant to be believed word for word. Some of it was written in the form of parables or allegories. The story of Adam and Eve and the Serpent, for example, was not meant to be believed exactly as it appeared in the Bible. It had been written to show that man had been given free will by God, so that when he did wrong—just as when he did right—it was by his own will. Among many other explanations, Moses wrote of the laws on sacrifice to God, that the sacrifice meant nothing in itself: what counted was the devotion to God and the sincerity of the prayers which accompanied the sacrifice.

The *Guide* made a very deep impression, not only on Jews but on Christians and Moslems as well. The argument that philosophy need not destroy religion persuaded many wavering Jews that if they studied philosophy, as they wanted to do, they would not lose their faith. When the *Guide* was translated into Latin it came to the notice of Christian philosophers and students of religion; and one of the greatest—Thomas Aquinas—used it as a model for his own writings. Moslem scholars were so impressed with the *Guide* that they wrote their own commentaries on it, and lectured on it to their students.

Some people disapproved of the *Guide* just as they had disapproved of the *Mishneh Torah*, but for rather different reasons. Every book which breaks entirely new ground and so disturbs an ancient tradition is censured; and the *Guide* was disliked by those teachers who feared and hated any kind of change. Some of them disliked the *Guide* so much that they forbade their students to read it; and everywhere it gave rise to heated discussion, argument and bitterness.

Moses Maimonides had kept aloof from the struggle, and when at length the arguments died away his book was recognized as valuable and sincere. He was not angry because people criticized him, for he respected opinions which differed from his own. Another of his works was his *Thirteen Articles of Faith*—thirteen principles of Judaism which could be used to show how Judaism differed from Christianity and Islam. The most important of these principles were those which stated the absolute oneness—or unity—of God, the Creator, the Eternal. God has no bodily substance, and if people picture Him in human form it is only because they cannot imagine Him in any other.

F

Although later scholars and philosophers were to describe some of the principles of Judaism rather differently from Maimonides, his *Thirteen Articles* are still remembered, for they form the basis of the well-known hymn, *Yigdal*, which is chanted in many synagogues today.

Moses Maimonides' ability to explain things clearly and simply meant that he understood the minds of ordinary people, and this helped to make him a good physician. He realized, as all good doctors do, that it is as vital to cure a sick mind as a sick body; and he knew how the mind can help or hinder the cure of the body. His fame as a doctor soon began to spread. Renowned physicians came to Cairo to consult with him, and he was made doctor at Saladin's court. The Sultan El-Adil, Saladin's brother, who ruled the country while Saladin was in Palestine fighting in the Third Crusade, was one of his patients; and it is said that Richard I, the Lion-hearted, wanted to consult him but that Maimonides declined the privilege.

In a long letter to a friend he described his busy daily life: it was obviously a life which he thoroughly enjoyed. He had to visit the Sultan every morning and if the Sultan or a member of his family was unwell Maimonides had to remain in Cairo all day. "It also frequently happens," he wrote, "that one or two of the royal officers fall sick, and I must attend to their healing. Hence, as a rule, I repair to Cairo very early in the day, and even if nothing unusual happens, I do not return to Fostat until the afternoon. Then I am almost dying with hunger."

At home he would find a crowd of patients awaiting him, Jews and non-Jews, rich people and poor.

"I dismount from my animal, wash my hands, go forth to my patients, and entreat them to bear with me while I partake of some slight refreshment, the only meal I take in the twenty-four hours. Then I attend to my patients, write prescriptions and directions for their various ailments." Consulting hours often went on far into the night, by which time the physician was so exhausted that he could scarcely speak.

The Sabbath was the only day on which he was free to advise his fellow-Jews. "On that day, the whole congregation, or, at least, the majority of the members, come to me after the morning service, when I instruct them as to their proceedings during the whole week. We study together a little until noon, when they depart. Some of them return and read with me after the afternoon service until evening prayers. In this manner I spend that day."

His duties as a physician and the important part he played in Jewish affairs would have been enough to fill the life of any ordinary man. But Moses Maimonides, who was extraordinarily energetic and never happy unless he was busy, was positively deluged with questions and requests for advice not only from the Jews of Cairo but from Jews from all over the world.

Then there were his writings. In addition to his main works, his writings included several books on medicine. Since he lived before the days of printing, the books—which were written in Arabic—were copied by hand. They were translated into Hebrew and into other languages; and after the invention of printing in the fifteenth century they were published and re-published many times. Moses Maimonides' ideas were far ahead of his times. Only about twenty years ago an article in a learned medical journal described one of his books, *A Treatise on Poisons and Antidotes*, as so up-to-date, scientific and practical that it might almost have been written in the twentieth century. And more recently still, in 1958, a new translation of one of his other books, on rules and regulations for keeping in good health, was commended for the knowledge it shows of the effect of the mind on the health of the body.

But to Jews, it is for his writings on Judaism that Moses Maimonides is best remembered, writings which made him the greatest of all the great Jewish writers of Spain; and which gave to his people a clear and simplified form of belief. He is also remembered for his work for the oppressed Jews of other lands. On one occasion, for example, the Jews of the Yemen in Arabia, who were being cruelly oppressed by the Moslems, wrote to him begging for advice as to what they should do. "Strengthen yourselves," he replied, "and let not the persecution frighten you, because that is only a test from God to see how strong your faith in Him is." But just as he had advised the Jews of Fez never to feel that they were idolaters if they did not accept martyrdom, so now he advised the Jews of the Yemen not to allow themselves to be killed but to leave the country, if they could, and settle elsewhere.

So, despite his bad health, Moses Maimonides continued to fill every minute of the day with work until he died, at the age of sixty-nine. His work has long outlived him; and although some of it has little bearing on the religious thought of today, much of the greatest importance and value remains. His studies and his work had served to strengthen his reverence for God. And it was for the quality of his faith as well as for his work that people sometimes compared him with Moses the great Law-giver. "From Moses to Moses"— so they put it—"there has been none like Moses."

ISAAC ABRAVANEL
(1437-1509)
The Loyal Statesman

For four centuries, as we have seen, Moorish Spain gave
shelter to the Jews. During those centuries scholarship
flourished and Jewish men of learning, physicians, financiers,
philosophers, poets and others played a distinguished part
in Spanish affairs. These four centuries, which produced in
Spain so rich a harvest of Jewish thought, are often spoken
of as the Golden Age.

By the beginning of the eleventh century there were
Jewish communities in nearly every other country in Europe;
but their lot was not so happy. The history of the Jews of
Europe in the Middle Ages is one of growing oppression and
misery. The leaders of the Catholic Church, fearful lest
Judaism should exercise any influence in Christian countries,
arranged for Jews to be excluded from all positions of
responsibility and, so far as possible, they kept Jews and
Christians apart. Jews were not allowed to own any land;
they were not allowed to become members of the Guilds
which had been formed to help and protect the various
trades.

The Jews had entered the countries of Europe as strangers;
and when they found that they could neither settle on the
land nor join a trade, they looked around for some other
means of support. Many of them took to commerce, buying

goods and selling them at a profit; while others became money-lenders, receiving interest on the money they lent. The Jews did not choose to become merchants or money-lenders: they took to these professions because no others were open to them.

As time passed and commerce prospered, the authorities decided that the Jews were becoming too successful: and the fear of Jewish influence became so strong that new laws and restrictions were continually being made to guard against it. Christians were forbidden by the Church to take service with infidels (and Jews, of course, were considered as infidels); they were forbidden to take any post which would make them subordinate to an infidel, or even to lodge in an infidel's house. To make sure that nobody had an excuse for transgressing these restrictions, infidels were ordered to wear a distinguishing badge. Thus publicly branded as infidels, the Jews drew more closely together. The towns had their Jewish quarters—or ghettoes. In these quarters the Jews lived and worshipped in their own synagogues; they studied the *Talmud* and the other sacred books; but they read no literature save their own, and they took no interest in non-Jewish affairs. The division which had been made between Christians and Jews put an end to friendship between them. It tended to make Christians dislike Jews; and it gave the Jews a narrow and restricted outlook at this period in history.

The inevitable result of the division was an ever-growing prejudice among Christians against anything Jewish; and as the years went by this prejudice turned into persecution. During the two hundred years of the Crusades (and there were eight Crusades between 1096 and 1271), infidels in Christian countries were killed in a series of massacres which turned the lives of the Jews into a nightmare of terror. The Crusaders who set out in 1096 to win Palestine from the Moslems paused in the Rhineland to massacre the Jewish infidels, who chose to die rather than to buy their lives by accepting baptism. In almost every country in Europe Jews were slain without mercy on the slightest pretext. And where no pretext existed, a false charge was invented against them. One of these charges was that the Jews slaughtered a Christian child as part of their Passover celebrations. The charge, of course, was entirely unfounded; but Christians believed it to be true, and it aroused in them an abiding hatred of the Jews and a longing for revenge.

Hatred led in the end to banishment. The first European country to expel the Jews was England. There had been Jews in England at the time of the Norman Conquest; and until 1189, when Richard the Lion-heart was crowned, they had been well enough treated. But Richard was himself a Crusader and, as we have heard, he led an army against the infidels of Palestine during the Third Crusade. Under Richard a wave of persecution broke over the Jews in England. It did not cease with Richard's death, but grew steadily stronger until in 1290 King Edward I expelled the Jews from the country. They went only as far as the nearest Continental countries, France and the Netherlands. But in France there was no peace; for France followed England's example and ordered the Jews to go. Germany did not actually expel them, but continued to reduce them by massacre. The German persecution reached a savage climax at the time of the Black Death, the plague which swept across Europe in the fourteenth century. The Jews in Germany were falsely accused of spreading the plague by poisoning the wells of drinking-water; and the accusation provided a pretext for fresh massacres. The Jews who survived began to flee the country. Some crossed the Alps into Italy: but the vast majority turned towards Poland, where Jews were being encouraged to settle.

In Spain, the Golden Age of the Jews had come to an end. By the close of the fourteenth century the whole of the Spanish peninsula (with the exception of Granada, which remained in Moslem hands) had become Christian. As Catholic influence strengthened, Christian prejudice hardened against those Jews who had survived Moslem oppression. In 1391 and again in 1411 waves of massacre swept across Spain. Among the Jews who survived were many who clung openly and defiantly to their faith. Others (less stout-hearted) had saved their lives by agreeing to be baptised into the Catholic Church. But, while outwardly they professed Christianity, they remained Jews at heart and in secret they continued to observe their own faith. These secret Jews, who called themselves New Christians, were known by genuine Christians as Maranos, a term which means "swine." Some of them prospered, gaining high positions in the army, at court and even in the Church.

But the Church remained suspicious of the loyalty of these New Christians: and when the Inquisition (the Roman Catholic ecclesiastical court set up to deal with charges of heresy) was introduced into Spain, it was directed principally against the unfortunate Maranos, although it was equally harsh with Christians deemed to be heretics. Any man who held opinions of which the Catholic Church disapproved was considered a heretic; and so every Jew who had been baptised but who was suspected of leanings towards his old faith, laid himself open to a charge of heresy. Spies were employed to watch the suspects; and on the slightest provocation a man would be arrested, dragged before the Inquisition and condemned without the shadow of a fair trial. A man who called himself a Christian might be observed to bless his children without making the sign of the cross: a simple action such as this could cause his arrest and trial. If he refused to plead guilty, torture was used on him to obtain a confession. Some Maranos, broken by pain, confessed to heresy and were pardoned after enduring the most humiliating penances. Others paid the penalty of their courage and, like the Christian "heretics," were burned to death at the stake. Under the Grand Inquisitor Torquemada this terrible penalty was enforced with the utmost severity.

It was after the first of the two waves of massacre—in 1391—that a distinguished family of Spanish Jews named Abravanel fled from Spain to Portugal. There had been a number of scholars and statesmen among the Abravanels; and the head of the family, who had posed as a Christian in Spain, returned to his own faith as soon as he had found sanctuary in Portugal. His son, Don Judah Abravanel, an exceedingly clever organizer and financier, was given a position in the household of one of the King of Portugal's sons; and by the time Don Judah's son, Isaac ben Jehudah Abravanel, was born in 1437 in Lisbon, the family had become prosperous and highly respected.

As a boy, Isaac Abravanel studied the history of Judaism as well as the usual subjects. He was keenly interested in religious literature and philosophy and he grew up to be deeply religious and extremely learned. But it was in practical ways rather than in scholarship that Isaac excelled. He possessed a quick and penetrating brain which gave him an easy mastery of figures and finance and of the complicated affairs of state. His ability was so outstanding that it brought him to the notice of the King, Alfonso V, who appointed him court treasurer and who, before long, was consulting him on all matters of state. Isaac Abravanel was very conscious of his good fortune. As he wrote many years later: "Tranquilly I lived in my inherited house in fair Lisbon. Thereto God had given me blessings, riches, and honour. I had built myself stately buildings and chambers. My house was the meeting-place of the learned and wise. I was reverenced in the palace of Alfonso, a mighty and upright king, under whom the Jews enjoyed freedom and prosperity. I was always at his side, was his support, and while he lived I went and came to his palace."

In his married life Don Isaac Abravanel was equally happy. He had a gracious and charming wife and three sturdy, intelligent sons. At court, he had formed close friendships with a number of influential Portuguese noblemen, who were glad to welcome him into their homes. But in this new life, with all its excitements, he never forgot that he was a Jew; and he was always ready to use his influence and his wealth in the service of his people.

But the good times were almost over. In 1481, when Don Isaac was forty-four, the kindly King Alfonso died and was succeeded by his son, Juan II. The new King was a proud and stern man, anxious at the beginning of his reign to strengthen his own position. For this he wanted money;

and, as his father's treasurer was a wealthy man, he cast eager eyes on the Jew's possessions. Warned by a Christian friend that his life as well as his property was in danger, Isaac and his family fled the country. They were only just in time. The King had given instructions that Don Isaac Abravanel was to be seized, dead or alive, and brought before him; and when he discovered that the treasurer had escaped he revenged himself by confiscating the whole of his property, his valuable books and manuscripts, including one which Don Isaac had been writing himself.

The Abravanel family found refuge with the Jewish community in the Spanish city of Toledo. Despite the desperate plight of the Maranos under the Inquisition, the Jews who had remained openly faithful to their religion had not yet suffered. As they had never pretended to be Christians, they could not be accused of heresy to the Church. The Jews of Toledo felt privileged to have among them so distinguished a scholar and statesman as Isaac Abravanel: and, now that he was no longer a statesman, Isaac turned his full attention to religious learning. He studied the *Torah*, and after a while began to write a commentary on the Prophets, a portion of the Bible which had hitherto been neglected. He was unable to finish the commentary at the time; but revised and completed it many years later, towards the end of his life.

He might have remained indefinitely writing and studying had his reputation as a financier not been so high. Ferdinand of Aragon, who ruled Spain jointly with his wife Isabella of Castile, needed money for a campaign he was planning against the Moslem kingdom of Granada. He had heard that Isaac Abravanel had proved himself a financial genius in Portugal; and so, summoning him to court, he placed the financial affairs of Spain in his hands. For ten years—from 1482 to 1492—Abravanel controlled the finances of Spain so brilliantly that he rescued the country from threatened bankruptcy. In return, the King rewarded him with many tokens of his esteem.

Once more Isaac became wealthy and prosperous; but in Spain, as in Portugal, he was always ready to help his own people. Some of his money he spent in another cause, a cause which was to change the whole face of the world. In 1492 the famous navigator Christopher Columbus prevailed on Ferdinand and Isabella to finance him in a voyage of discovery. Some of Columbus' chief supporters were Jews and Maranos, and among them was Isaac Abravanel, who contributed towards the expenses of the expedition. A number of the sailors who sailed with Columbus were Jews or Maranos; the maps which he used had been drawn by Jewish mapmakers; and so it is true to say that, but for Jewish help, the discovery of the New World could not have been made so soon.

Columbus sailed in 1492. At the very beginning of the year, after a lengthy war, the Moslem kingdom of Granada had fallen to the Christian invaders. On January 2nd, Ferdinand and Isabella made a triumphant entry into the beautiful city of Granada, amidst the pealing of bells and the shouts of rejoicing which greeted the end of Islam in the Iberian peninsula. The fall of Granada proved a disaster to the Jews. People began to speak of the campaign as a holy war against the infidels. The infidel Moslems had been vanquished, they declared, so why should the infidel Jews be allowed to go free? Under Torquemada's reign of terror about a third of all the Maranos had already perished. But this was not enough for the Grand Inquisitor: he was determined to rid Spain of the Jews, the openly orthodox ones as well as the Maranos.

Until this time the King and Queen had given little support to the Inquisition in its persecution of Marano heretics; but with the fall of Granada, where a number of Maranos had taken refuge, they began to waver. Torquemada now insisted that it was their duty to expel the Jews: he argued and pressed them until in the end they gave way. On March 31st, 1492, from the Alhambra, the ancient palace of the Moorish kings of Granada, Ferdinand and Isabella issued a decree that every Jew must leave Spain and the Spanish possessions, within four months, on pain of death. They might take with them only their personal possessions:

their money and their property would all be confiscated by the state. The only excuse for the issue of this cruel edict was the loyalty of the Jews to their own faith. By their noble example they were encouraging the Maranos to throw off the guise of Christianity and return openly to Judaism.

When they realized what the edict meant, the Jews turned for help to the only Jew who had influence at court—Don Isaac Abravanel. Hastening to the King and Queen, Abravanel implored them to revoke the edict. His Christian friends—Spanish noblemen—supported his petition; and when he saw that it had failed he flung himself on his knees and offered the King and Queen a vast sum of money in exchange for the safety of his people. Ferdinand, in need of money as usual, was tempted. But as he hesitated Torquemada, who had been warned of what was afoot, entered the audience chamber to rebuke the King and Queen for their disloyalty to the Catholic faith. Holding aloft a crucifix he exclaimed: "Judas Iscariot sold Christ for thirty pieces of silver. Are your Majesties ready to sell him for three hundred thousand ducats? Here he is; sell him!"

With this taunt the fate of three hundred thousand Jews was sealed. Ferdinand and Isabella had been shamed out of revoking the edict; and on August 2nd it was put into effect. To the very last the Jews were given a choice between banishment and conversion, but scarcely any of them chose baptism. A few Maranos who had contrived to hoodwink the Inquisition stayed on, and at the risk of their lives continued to observe their faith in secret and to teach it to their children. The remainder, in sorrow and anxiety, left the country of their birth, the country which had sheltered their ancestors for generations.

The majority of the fugitives took the road to Portugal. They suffered intensely from weariness and hunger; and on the way they were attacked by bandits who robbed and murdered them for their poor possessions. For those who survived Portugal offered only a temporary refuge; for in 1496 the King of Portugal, following Ferdinand and Isabella's example, issued a decree bidding all Jews and other unbelievers to leave the country within ten months. In actual fact, very few of them left. Unwilling to lose such hardworking people, the King ordered the mass baptism of all Jewish children. Rather than submit, many Jews killed first their children and then themselves; while the survivors were imprisoned and tortured into submission.

Portugal had not been the only goal for the Spanish Jews. A few of the fugitives had managed to reach Palestine, others had got as far as Italy, where for a time they were allowed to settle in peace. The Turkish Empire also became a refuge for exiled Jews, and so did parts of North Africa and Holland.

Isaac Abravanel and his family had journeyed to Naples (then an independent kingdom). The King of Naples was a friend to the Jews. He welcomed the distinguished Jewish statesman and made him his adviser, raising him once again to high office. But Naples was captured by the French in 1495. The King, forced to abdicate, fled to Messina in Sicily; and with him went Isaac Abravanel, who, alone among the King's ministers, had remained loyal to him.

Within a few months the King died in exile. "My wife and sons are away from me, in another country," wrote Abravanel, "and I am left by myself, alone, an alien in a strange land." But Don Isaac was not the sort of man to give way to despair, and, as once before, he found comfort in study. Soon he started to write, using his knowledge of modern history and affairs of state as well as his knowledge of the Bible and Judaism. His understanding of modern history enabled him to judge the influence of ancient history on the people and literature of Biblical times; and the books he wrote became very popular.

When the French left Naples (and they did not hold it for very long), Abravanel returned to continue his writing. The intense sympathy he felt for his people in their exile caused his thoughts to dwell more and more on the idea of a Messiah. One day, so Jews believed, the Messiah, the deliverer appointed by God, would reunite the exiles, lead them rejoicing back to Palestine, and open a Messianic age of faith, peace and happiness. In the darkness of exile the thought of the Messiah was a beam of light and hope. A number of Jewish writers had already written of him (Moses Maimonides among them), and some had even claimed knowledge of the actual date of his coming. More than once a man had arisen who declared himself to be the appointed leader. Each of these false Messiahs drew a large following of eager, hopeful Jews. But one by one they were exposed as frauds; and all they achieved was the added misery and despair of the people they had duped. Despite these false leaders, belief in the Messiah persisted; and in three of his books Isaac Abravanel sought to sustain and strengthen his people with his conviction that the true Messiah would one day appear.

The closing years of Abravanel's own life were happy ones. In 1503, at the age of sixty-five, his second son, Isaac, who was a physician, had invited his father to come and share his home in Venice. In Venice the old man was caught up yet again into affairs of state and was often consulted. Isaac Abravanel was a foreigner and a Jew; but in spite of this he was asked by the government to negotiate a treaty on the spice trade between the Republic of Venice and Portugal, the country of his birth.

Although his wife was now dead, Don Isaac was happy in his three sons. The eldest, Judah Leon Medigo, a distinguished physician, scientist and mathematician who had settled in Genoa, came to Venice to spend several years with his father. The youngest son, Samuel, held an important post at the court of Naples. Like his father, Samuel Abravanel was devoted to his faith and his people; and in his public life he showed much of his father's loyalty, honesty and integrity.

When Isaac Abravanel died in the summer of 1509 at the age of seventy-two Christians as well as Jews paid tribute to him as a true and stalwart friend. Had he lived another year he would have seen his son Samuel and Samuel's wife, Donna Benvenida, intervene, as he himself had once intervened, in a desperate bid to stay an edict of expulsion, this time from Naples. They succeeded, though not absolutely or for long; for a few years later such harsh laws were introduced that the Jews were thankful to leave the country. Once they had gone they were not allowed to return; and in 1540 those Jews who had remained in Naples were driven out. Italy was no longer safe, and by the end of the century the Jews had also been driven out of the Republic of Genoa and the Duchy of Milan. By the beginning of the seventeenth century the whole of Western Europe, save for parts of Northern Italy and a few regions in Germany, was closed to the Jews.

JOSEPH NASI

(d. 1579)

Adviser to the Sultan of Turkey

WHEN Catholic Spain expelled the Jews in 1492, their plight would indeed have been desperate but for the friendship of the Moslem world. In the past, as we have seen, Jews had been both befriended and persecuted by Islam; and now, at the moment of their direst need, Moslem Turkey lay open to them. The Sultan of Turkey, an enlightened man, realized that his country would benefit from the entry of Jewish scholars and teachers, physicians and scientists, merchants, farmers and artisans. "You call Ferdinand a wise king?" he exclaimed. "Why, he has made his country poor and enriched ours by these useful subjects!"

Some of the most pious Jews—those who thought only of reviving the spirit of learning and religion in the Holy Land—contrived to return to Palestine; but the majority of the exiles who survived the horrors of the journey came to Turkey. Despite an occasional outbreak of enmity towards them, they soon settled down and became, as the Sultan had prophesied, extremely useful subjects.

The most useful of them was born early in the sixteenth century (the exact date is unknown), in a Spanish Marano family. The Hebrew name of the family was Nasi, but as Maranos they called themselves Miquez. In order to escape the Inquisition they fled to Portugal, where the father of the family, a physician by profession, became doctor to the King. His son, Joseph Nasi, grew up as a Jew in secret. He chafed against the necessity of hiding his religion; but in Portugal by this time, as in Spain, Maranos were in constant danger from the Inquisition, which had been introduced in 1531. Other members of the Miquez family felt as Joseph did, particularly his aunt, the widow of his eldest uncle, who was called Beatrice da Luna in Portugal but whose real name was Gracia Mendes. When Joseph was old enough to make up his mind, he decided to leave Portugal with his aunt and her family and go to Antwerp in Flanders. On the way they paid a short visit to England; and there they found that, despite the ban on Jews, a small number of Marano families were living, Christians in name but Jews in private. Religious services were held in the house of one of them; and fugitives from Europe were given assistance and advice.

Donna Gracia and her nephew had decided to settle in Antwerp because there was a branch of the family banking firm of Mendes in the city. Joseph, a handsome, charming and exceedingly clever young man, joined the firm; and soon, like other members of the family, made many Christian friends. His appearance and his manners made him very popular with the nobility; and he became a favourite at the court of the Queen Regent of the Netherlands.

But Flanders at the time was Spanish territory; and in Antwerp, as in Portugal, Joseph was obliged to conceal his religion. He therefore decided to leave Antwerp and take advantage of the Sultan's offer to settle in Turkey. With him in the plan was his aunt, a most devout woman, who longed to proclaim her faith openly. Gracia Mendes was a really great woman. She was generous and sincere, courageous and selfless, a woman to whom people turned instinctively for help. She had only one child, a most beautiful daughter named Reyna, so beautiful that she had many suitors, among them a courtier of the Queen Regent. The Queen sent for Donna Gracia and told her that she herself would arrange the marriage; to which Donna Gracia replied outspokenly that she would sooner see her daughter dead.

This remark was naturally taken as an insult. Donna Gracia had made it at an unfortunate moment. There was growing suspicion of the Maranos throughout the Low Countries; and she had provided the money to smuggle a number of Maranos out of Spain and the hands of the Inquisition.

It therefore seemed advisable to go at once. With some difficulty the fugitives made their way through France and reached the Republic of Venice. In Venice news leaked out that Donna Gracia was taking the family fortune to Turkey and that as soon as she arrived there she intended to revert openly to her own faith. Bent on gaining possession of the fortune, the authorities of the Republic arrested Donna Gracia, seized her property, and put her in prison on a charge of a relapse into Judaism. Her nephew Joseph, seriously alarmed, made a moving appeal to the Sultan of Turkey, Suleiman, and convinced him that it would be much to Turkey's advantage to welcome so distinguished and wealthy a woman. The Sultan responded by sending emissaries to Venice to demand Donna Gracia's release and the restoration of her property. Discussions dragged on for two years before the Venetian authorities agreed to the Sultan's demands and Donna Gracia was told she might go. The Sultan sent a special messenger to escort her and her daughter Reyna to Constantinople, where they were received with great kindness.

In Constantinople, a Jewess now in name as well as in faith, Donna Gracia set to work for her own people. When she learned that the Maranos of Ancona in Italy (among them some Jewish businessmen from Turkey) had been flung into prison on a charge of heresy, she appealed to the Sultan to intervene with the Pope. The Sultan wrote a stern letter demanding that his Jewish subjects be released forthwith, and threatening that if anything happened to them he would take his revenge on the Christians who lived in his dominions. Alarmed for the safety of the Christians, the Pope ordered the release of the Turkish Jews. Had the

Sultan been able to do so, he would have demanded the release of all the prisoners; but he was, of course, powerless to help any but his own subjects.

Donna Gracia's nephew, who had followed her to Turkey, publicly discarded the name of Miquez and assumed his Hebrew name of Joseph Nasi; and then, to his aunt's joy, Joseph and the lovely Reyna were married. Donna Gracia and Joseph launched many schemes for the relief of their people. They gave money to the poor; founded houses of prayer and schools for the study of the *Talmud*, giving generously to provide teachers and books.

Joseph Nasi did not remain long in the background, and the story of his career in Turkey reads like a fairy tale. In Spain he would probably have been burnt as a heretic: in Turkey, with its growing population of Jews, he became second only to the Sultan himself. Suleiman had been quick to see his ability and to recognize the value to Turkey of his knowledge of Christian Europe. He promoted this new and brilliant subject to the highest office, placing him in charge of Turkey's foreign affairs.

Ambassadors from Europe now had to swallow their hatred of Joseph as a Jew and treat him as an equal. They had to ask his advice and, on occasion, beg him to intercede with the Sultan on their behalf. His influence on the foreign affairs of Turkey became so powerful that when the appointment of a new king for Poland was being debated, it was Joseph Nasi who swayed the election; and, in return, gained from the king a promise of protection for the Jews. He also encouraged the Protestant Netherlands to revolt against Catholic Spain, although he was unable to persuade the Sultan to declare war on Spain. He did, however, persuade him to declare war on the Republic of Venice (perhaps because the Jews of Venice had suffered so grievously), as a result of which Turkey gained possession of the island of Cyprus. When the Jews were driven out of the greater part of Italy, they turned to Joseph Nasi, knowing that the most powerful man in Turkey was their friend and protector and that in the Turkish Empire they would find a home.

When Suleiman died his son, Selim, who succeeded him, continued to hold Joseph Nasi in the highest esteem. He appointed him a member of his personal bodyguard; and more than this, created him Duke of Naxos and the islands of the Cyclades. The respect in which Joseph of Naxos was held in the East reminded his fellow Jews of that other Joseph of ancient times at the court of Egypt.

The reward which pleased him most, and which was given him during Suleiman's lifetime, was the gift of a tract of land in Palestine on the Sea of Tiberias. For years Joseph had dreamed of founding a Jewish state. In Venice, a fugitive Marano, he had even dared to plead with the Republic to people one of its many islands with Jews. His plea had been rejected: but now, with this gift of land and with the wealth of his generous mother-in-law, his dream could be made to come true. Joseph immediately issued a proclamation to the oppressed Jews of Europe offering them a home and protection in Palestine if, in return, they would agree to work as farmers and artisans. The tract of land he had been given included the ruined city of Tiberias and seven villages; and Joseph instructed one of his agents to organize the rebuilding of the city. Selim gave orders that the Arab inhabitants of nearby villages should help; with incredible swiftness houses and streets were constructed, and within a year a new and beautiful city had come into being. Joseph planned to make Tiberias a manufacturing town, a competitor of wealthy Venice. He ordered mulberry trees to be planted for the manufacture of silk; and he imported wool from Spain for the weaving of fine cloth.

The Jewish population of Palestine, enriched by the scholarly exiles from Spain, was regaining the great qualities which had been sadly lacking when Moses Maimonides had visited the Holy Land. The little colony of Tiberias might have been an added source of strength; but almost before it had come into being its founder lost interest in it. Joseph of Naxos, who had gained more awards and titles than any professing Jew since ancient times, had set his heart on yet another prize: his ambition was to become King of Cyprus, now a Turkish possession. Joseph may well have planned to turn the island of Cyprus into a Jewish community; but he was not offered the crown, and his dream of an independent Jewish state vanished. Perhaps he allowed his disappointment over Cyprus to destroy his interest in Tiberias: perhaps he was simply one of those brilliant and energetic people, restless and easily bored, who dash from one project to another, interested only in the most recent.

As he grew older his enormous influence began to wane. Selim died in 1574; and although his son, Murad III, respected his father's dying request that the Jew should be left in possession of his rank and office, the new Sultan never turned to him for advice. The elderly Joseph found himself cold-shouldered and ignored. He did not live long, but died in 1579, only five years after Salim, whom he had served so well.

It is true that Joseph of Naxos, renowned in his time, had accomplished no lasting good for Judaism. Rabbis and scholars have left us a legacy of faith and learning; but Joseph was not a scholar. He was a diplomat and a man of the world; and his work was confined to his own day. Everywhere, however, his people were heartened by the thought that, while the Jews had been thrust low in the Christian world, in Islam a professing Jew had risen to be the most esteemed of the Sultan's ministers. This knowledge was like a light in the darkness. It filled the unhappy Jews of Europe with hope that, where Joseph of Naxos had led, other Jews would follow.

MENASSEH BEN ISRAEL
(1604-1657)
The Founder of Anglo-Jewry

ALTHOUGH exiled Jews from Spain had found shelter in Moslem Turkey by the opening of the seventeenth century, most of Western Europe was still barred to them. But to a great many of the fugitives Turkey seemed impossibly far away—an eastern world, entirely different from the civilization they knew. Even worse than the plight of the professing Jews was the plight of the Maranos, the "New Christians" who had decided to take the risk of remaining in the land of their birth. The Inquisition, which Protestants and Maranos had trusted would vanish with the death of Torquemada in 1498, had flared up again under King Philip II, the King whose vaunted Armada was defeated by the English in 1588. Once again heretics (Protestants and Maranos) were tortured and burned in the name of Christianity. Some of the Maranos had become both wealthy and influential, but their influence could not protect them from the Inquisition if they were suspected of Jewish practices; and so most of them decided on flight. In Europe there was one country which would not only shelter but welcome them—Holland. After a gallant struggle against the rule by Catholic Spain, the Protestant Dutch had gained their independence; and under William of Orange (known as William the Silent) the spirit of religious freedom and tolerance had been established.

The Maranos of Spain and Portugal—scholars and physicians, statesmen and merchants—now hastened to Holland. There, at long last, they could proclaim their Jewish faith, build themselves a synagogue, found schools and charitable institutions for their poor. The Dutch treated them as important guests, proud of the ability, the knowledge and wealth which was now at the service of their country; and very soon Dutch scholars were coming to Jewish scholars for guidance on the interpretation of the Bible and the study of Hebrew.

Oppressed Jews from other countries were also fleeing to Holland, particularly Jews from Germany and Poland. Although Germany had never expelled the Jews, through the centuries they had been oppressed and persecuted. Jewish fugitives from Germany, as we know, had been well received in Poland; and by the middle of the sixteenth century the Jewish community in Poland was large and flourishing. The Jews of Poland had been kindly treated. They had been allowed to trade and to farm, and to act as stewards and tax collectors on the nobles' estates. Things had gone well for them until in 1648 the Cossacks of the Ukraine, under a leader named Chmielnicki, revolted against the bad government of their Polish overlords. Because the Jews had been working and acting for the nobles, the Cossacks turned on them in frenzy. They tortured and killed the Jews in a series of massacres more dreadful than any that had occurred since the massacres in Germany at the time of the Black Death. Some of the survivors, dazed and terrified, succeeded in escaping to Holland, where they were joined by refugees from Germany.

Except for their faith, the German and Polish Jews had almost nothing in common with the refugees from Spain and Portugal. Many of them had been born and had spent their lives herded together in ghettoes—or Jewish quarters. They spoke different languages; their customs were different; and they lacked the culture and polish of the Spanish and Portuguese Jews. Nevertheless, they were thrifty, hard-working, and eager to learn; and they, too, found a ready welcome and a new life in Holland.

Holland's example was followed before very long by other European countries. When, for example, the King of Denmark realized that the Jewish outcasts were actually conferring benefits on their new country, he made it known that his territories were open to the Jews. So also did two independent rulers, the Dukes of Modena and of Savoy. In England and France, however, no such move was made.

About the year 1604, some forty years before the Chmielnicki massacres brought peace for the Jews of Poland to a violent end, a boy was born whose name—Menasseh ben Israel—will always be revered by the Jews of Britain. Joseph ben Israel, the boy's father, was a Portuguese Marano who had been tortured by the Inquisition and had emerged from prison without money or possessions and ruined in health. As soon as he was sufficiently recovered, Joseph took his family to Amsterdam; and Menasseh, his youngest son, was probably born during the journey.

In Amsterdam Joseph found a large and growing Jewish community. Despite ill health, he set himself to the study of Hebrew and of the Judaism and the Jewish way of life he was free in Holland to follow. He never recovered his health and he remained very poor; but his son Menasseh, a most promising boy, was given a good education and a thorough grounding in Hebrew. Under the finest teachers of the day he studied the Bible and the *Talmud* and developed the remarkable gift he possessed for languages. At the age of fifteen the boy could preach a sermon: at seventeen he wrote the first of many books, a Hebrew grammar which he called *Clear Language*. He was only eighteen when he was appointed a preacher in one of Amsterdam's synagogues and a teacher in the school.

Joseph ben Israel lived just long enough to see his youngest son launched on his career. He died in 1622; and his wife did not long survive him. His parents' death left Menasseh feeling very desolate. He was living with an older brother and sister when he met the young woman who shortly afterwards became his wife. Her name was Rachel; and she was a great-granddaughter of the famous statesman Isaac Abravanel. The Abravanel family claimed to be descended from King David; and when in due course two sons and a daughter were born to Menasseh and Rachel, the proud father used to boast that his children were of royal descent.

Whether or not they were descended from David, the children were born at a time when their father was hard put to it to support them. Menasseh had married very young; and now, in order to make both ends meet, he became a printer as well as a rabbi and teacher, and set up the first Hebrew printing-press in Holland. Even so, he was not earning enough, and he began to think seriously of throwing up his career and of emigrating to the New World as a merchant. Maranos had been living in the New World since the middle of the sixteenth century; for one of the penalties paid by New Christians who, under torture and the threat of death, had "repented" of their heresy was deportation to the Portuguese colony of Brazil.

By this time professing Jews were living openly in Brazil; and in Pernambuco, where Menasseh ben Israel's brother had settled, there was quite a large Jewish community. Menasseh was at work on another book at the time. Written in Spanish, the book, which he called *The Conciliator*, set out to compose the differences in those passages in the Bible which seemed to conflict with one another. When it was finished Menasseh dedicated the second part to the Jews of Pernambuco.

He never went to Brazil, however. In the nick of time two wealthy members of his congregation came to the conclusion that Menasseh ben Israel was far too valuable a rabbi to be lost to Amsterdam. They therefore founded a college and offered Menasseh the post of principal. He accepted; for the salary was large enough for him to keep his family and the work gave him leisure to preach and to write—the two pursuits he loved best.

Menasseh's books, interesting and easy to read, were

exceedingly popular. Menasseh himself cannot be counted among the great Jewish scholars, because he made no new discoveries and added nothing fresh to the knowledge of the day. He wrote with such fluency and ease (and he was equally at home in half a dozen languages) that some of his books were too hurriedly put together and lacked real thought. But they aroused a great deal of interest among Christian scholars in the literature of the *Talmud* and the Jewish point of view; and they gained for Menasseh the admiration and friendship of Christians as well as Jews.

Among the most famous of Menasseh's friends was Queen Christina of Sweden. She was a learned woman who tried, but failed, to persuade her government to admit the Jews to Sweden. Another friend was the great artist Rembrandt. Rembrandt made an etching of Menasseh, showing him with a strong but kindly face, dark-eyed and broad-cheeked, with a moustache and narrow beard hiding the lines of his mouth. He dressed very soberly; and the etching shows him wearing the dark, wide-brimmed hat of the period and a wide white collar over his dark clothes.

Menasseh was a very friendly man, warm-hearted, honest and straightforward, with a simple but charming manner which helped to win him many Jewish and Christian friends. He felt a special sympathy for the sufferings of his own people; and this made him study with enthusiasm everything that had been written about the coming of the Messiah and of the Messianic age. Like his wife's great-grandfather, Isaac Abravanel, and other Jewish scholars, Menasseh had read carefully all the passages in the Bible which referred, however indirectly, to the subject. And, like them, he believed in the absolute truth of every word he read. In the Book of Deuteronomy he had read the warning that God's people would be scattered "from one end of the earth even unto the other"; and in the Book of Daniel of scattering "the power of the holy people." He felt certain that only after the Jews had been scattered to every corner of the world would the promised Messiah come to reunite them and lead them back to the Holy Land.

It was just about this time that he met a Marano who had recently returned from a visit to South America with some amazing stories. In 1641, the Marano declared, he had come upon some Red Indians who followed certain Jewish customs and ceremonials and who belonged without doubt to the lost Hebrew Tribes of Reuben and Levi. Menasseh ben Israel was quite sure that he was speaking the truth and that the American Indians did indeed belong to the Tribes which had been dispersed after the destruction of Jerusalem and the Temple in 586 BCE. He used the Marano's tale in one of his books, tracing the route of these Red Indian "Jews" from Central Asia through China to South America. In the book, which he called *The Hope of Israel*, and which was published in 1650, Menasseh argued that the Jews were already scattered over the greater part of the world; and that when they were allowed to enter the countries which still refused to admit them, the conditions would be fulfilled and the Messiah would appear. His own hopes turned towards England, which in medieval Jewish literature was described as *kenaf haaretz*, meaning "the end of the earth." If England, then, would admit the Jews, Menasseh was convinced that the prophecy of the coming of the Messiah would indeed come to pass. It might not matter if one or two other countries refused to allow them in, provided England— "the end of the earth"—lifted the centuries-old ban.

The mystery of the lost Tribes of Israel was one in which Christians as well as Jews were deeply interested, chief among them the Puritans of England. For many years (as Donna Gracia Mendes had discovered) a very small Marano colony had existed in England which, by the middle of the seventeenth century, numbered about 200 people. The Maranos, of course, professed Christianity but practised their Judaism in secret; for no orthodox Jew had been allowed to enter the country since the expulsion in 1290. Menasseh ben Israel, who thought quite rightly that the Puritans would sympathize with him, sent a copy of *The Hope of Israel* to the English Parliament. With the book he sent a letter begging that the Jews should no longer be prevented from making a home for themselves in England, and offering to come to England himself and present his plea to Parliament.

He had chosen his time with the greatest care. The Puritan party under Oliver Cromwell had been in power since 1648; and Cromwell and his men drew their inspiration from the heroes of the Old Testament. Cromwell was fond of comparing himself with heroes like Gideon and Judas Maccabeus who had liberated their people from the tyrants of old, just as *he* had destroyed in England the power of the Stuart Kings. Oliver Cromwell was made Lord Protector of England in 1653; and in Puritan England there was a return to the teachings of the Bible, particularly to the teachings of the Old Testament. There were many Puritans who had the greatest admiration for the Jewish people as well as for Jewish thought. They used Biblical phrases in ordinary conversation: some gave their children Hebrew names: and some even went as far as to call themselves Jews and refer to the rule of the Stuarts as "the Egyptian Bondage."

To Menasseh ben Israel it seemed obvious that, in a country so friendly towards the Jews, the next step must be to readmit them. A number of well-known Englishmen thought so too. One of them wrote a treatise in which he claimed that the suffering which had been caused in England by the Civil War (which had ended in victory for Oliver Cromwell and was followed by the execution of King Charles I) was a just punishment for England's treatment of the Jews. Englishmen, the writer continued, must atone for their sin by admitting the Jews and treating them as brothers.

This treatise, and other indications of Puritan goodwill, was a sign to Menasseh that his plea would be heard with sympathy. And so it was; for he received an invitation to come to England and appear before Parliament. He was ready to go when war broke out between England and Holland; and it was impossible for him to leave Amsterdam until peace had been declared.

He had no idea that the Dutch Government would raise any objections to his plan; but object they did in terms which he found most flattering. Holland, Menasseh was informed, had no intention of allowing her Jews to leave and settle elsewhere, particularly in England, her chief rival. Menasseh quietened suspicion by explaining that he was only seeking a refuge in England for oppressed Jews from other countries; and that the Jews of Holland were proud to think that their presence was valued.

Menasseh arrived in London in mid-September, 1655, and took lodgings in the Strand. With him were three Rabbis, one of whom—Jacob Sasportas—was later to become *Haham* (which in Hebrew means "sage") or Chief Rabbi of the first London community of Jews. New Year fell a few days after Menasseh's arrival; and for the first time since 1290 the festival was celebrated in London, openly and with due ceremony.

Immediately afterwards Menasseh published a pamphlet. In it he begged Oliver Cromwell to readmit the Jews; to abolish all the ancient laws against them; and to allow the Maranos to return openly to the practice of their Jewish faith.

The pamphlet created a sensation. Some people argued for it, others against. There were still many Englishmen who disliked and feared the Jews. City merchants were afraid of Jewish competition. Clergymen, who held the Jews of the world responsible for the crucifixion of Jesus (and to Christians Jesus has always been the Messiah), were afraid of Jewish influence and terrified lest Jews should try and convert Christians to Judaism.

The merits of the case were still being debated violently when, on November 12th, Menasseh ben Israel delivered his petition to the Lord Protector. In the petition, and in the pamphlet, he stated the case for the readmission of the Jews with dignity and restraint. He asked for justice, not mercy; and wisely he stressed the benefits or "profit" which the Jews would confer on England. He spoke of their industry and ability, of their skill in "merchandizing" which would be at England's disposal. And he made it clear that the Jews would not come to England as visitors who planned to get rich and then to take their money back to their own country. If the Jews were admitted, their profits would remain in the country, for England would be their home.

Menasseh's appeal and his sincere and upright bearing made a deep impression on the Lord Protector. Cromwell believed that the Jews should be admitted, and he resolved to push the petition through his Council of State. A motion was therefore introduced: "That the Jews deserving it may be admitted into this nation to trade and traffic and dwell among us." The motion was not carried, as Cromwell had hoped. Instead, a committee was appointed to consider it; and the committee decided to canvass public opinion and to call a National Conference.

This decision gave rise to a crop of the most fantastic stories. One of the most ridiculous was that the Jews had offered Parliament half a million pounds to buy St. Paul's Cathedral in order to turn it into a synagogue. Another was that the Jews believed that Oliver Cromwell was their promised Messiah. Meanwhile, all the old false accusations against the Jews were revived. They were accused of being misers and usurers. They were accused of shedding the blood of a Christian child at their Passover celebrations: of idolatry before the scrolls of the Law: of mocking and cursing at other religions: and of aiming to convert all Christians to Judaism.

These false accusations were first made separately and then brought together in a pamphlet which was widely read and believed. To this pamphlet Menasseh ben Israel was invited to reply. He did so in what today is the best known of his writings, a pamphlet called *Vindiciae Judaeorum—Defence of the Jews*. In it Menasseh denied and refuted the false accusations and described the grandeur of Judaism and the demands which it makes. When, for example, he dealt with the charge that Jews were usurers, he explained that Judaism expects in all the affairs of everyday life honesty and upright dealings. But if, he said, "notwithstanding, there be some that do contrary to this, they do it not as Jewes simply but as wicked Jewes." He ended with an earnest and humble request to the people of England to consider his arguments "impartially, without prejudice and devoid of all passion."

The fiercest passions had, however, been aroused; and ignorant or bigoted people continued to believe all the false charges. The National Conference met five times without coming to a definite decision. At the final meeting Cromwell expressed his feelings so clearly and frankly that some one who was present said afterwards: "I never heard a man speak so well."

When the committee which had summoned the National Conference reported back to the Council of State it did, in fact, recommend that the Jews should be readmitted on certain stringent conditions. But the Council of State rejected the recommendation, although they agreed that the Maranos who had already settled in England should come to no harm so long as they continued to observe their Judaism in private.

This agreement proved to be the thin edge of the wedge. The Maranos of England—fugitives from Spain—were still officially Spanish subjects. In 1656 England was at war with Spain; and the Government decided to confiscate all the property of Spaniards resident in England. This measure would leave the Maranos completely penniless. And so they drew up a petition to Cromwell which was signed, among others, by Menasseh ben Israel, asking permission to live in England, not as Spaniards but as members of the Jewish nation. The petition was granted. Although it did not give permission for the Jews to return, it recognized the existence of the Maranos as Jews.

This was a most important concession. The Maranos of England (or Jews as they may now be called) were free to worship openly; and in December, 1656, they rented a house in Creechurch Lane, in the City of London, which they used as a synagogue. A few months later they rented a piece of ground for use as a cemetery; for until then the dead had been buried in consecrated ground in private gardens or else taken to Holland for burial. The house and ground were the first signs that the presence of Jews in England was an accepted fact. It was only a matter of time before these openly professing Jews were joined by others.

Menasseh ben Israel did not live to see this happen. Although his *Defence of the Jews* had won the approval of enlightened people, his petition had not succeeded and he believed that his mission had been a failure. Cromwell had given him a pension, and he stayed on in England, vainly seeking support for the cause; but the Lord Protector was too busy with other problems to allow him to renew his petition. In the autumn of 1657 Menasseh's son Samuel, who was with him, died; and Menasseh took his body back to Holland for burial. He never returned to England; but himself died at the age of fifty-three two months later.

Menasseh ben Israel was buried near the grave of his father Joseph. His epitaph was written, in Hebrew and Spanish, on a plain white headstone: "He is not dead; for in heaven he lives in supreme glory whilst on earth his pen has won him immortal remembrances." But it is as a man of action rather than as a writer that we remember Menasseh today. Although he died in the belief that he had failed, the Jews of Britain look on him rightly as their founder. His character and the single-mindedness with which he had pursued his mission had made a lasting impression on many influential Englishmen; and nobody who knew him personally could believe that the false accusations made about the Jews were true.

Within a year of his death Jews were living openly in London: within ten years London had a large Jewish community, despite the fact that Parliament had not yet officially given permission for the Jews to return. And England treated the Jews well, although she had not yet granted them the rights of English citizens. Menasseh ben Israel had dreamed of an open and triumphant return of the Jews; and his dream had been realized, though indirectly. During the 300 years which have passed since that time the Jews have been granted the privileges and the responsibilities of free and equal citizenship. In return, the British Jews have played, and continue to play, a full and respected part in the life of the country.

MOSES MENDELSSOHN
(1729-1786)
Leader of Germany's Jews

I N England and in Holland by the opening of the eighteenth
century Jews had been accepted as useful citizens; and
all over the New World, particularly in the British and Dutch
colonies, Jewish settlements were forming. But although the
influence of the Inquisition, under which Protestants and
Maranos had suffered so grievously, had begun to wane, the
Jews still existed only on sufferance in most of the countries
of Europe. In Germany their plight was especially hard. In
the cities where they lived they were herded into ghettoes, and
if they ventured into the streets beyond they were jeered at
or stoned. Only the meanest occupations were open to them.
They could not own land or farm: they could hold no sort of
public office; and the professions, trades, and the universities
were barred to them. It is true that in England there still
existed restrictions which prevented Jews and Roman
Catholics from holding certain offices and kept them out of
Parliament and the universities. But there were no ghettoes in
England. The Jews were not hounded and despised, they
were free; and, like all free men and women, they had
dignity and a proper sense of pride.

The harsh treatment meted out to the Jews of Germany
had robbed them of all dignity and pride. As far as possible,
they kept out of sight and made themselves inconspicuous in

an effort to avoid trouble. In their bitter humiliation they clung together and took no interest at all in the life beyond the ghetto walls. When they had to venture out they slunk along with bowed heads. Because there seemed no future for them in the outside world they made a world for themselves in the ghetto.

In these unhappy conditions, in the Jewish quarter of Dessau, capital of the state of Anhalt, a delicate baby boy was born to Menachem Mendel and his wife. The Mendels lived in a poor little house in a mean street, for Menachem Mendel, who was a scribe, earned a tiny wage by copying scrolls of the Law. The sickly baby was named Moses Mendelssohn (the son of Mendel), but his fellow Jews called him Moses Dessau.

As he grew into childhood the boy began to show very great promise, and his parents gave him the best education they could afford. When he had learned all his father could teach him he went to a ghetto school. His parents were worried about his health, for he had remained delicate; and there is a story that in the cold winter months his mother would wrap him up in a warm old cloak of her own and his father would carry him in a bundle to school. The subjects taught in the ghetto schools were mostly those connected with religion; and at a very early age Moses was promoted to the study of the *Talmud*. By a stroke of luck he had as his teacher David Frankel, the Rabbi of Dessau, who was a distinguished scholar. Under Rabbi Frankel Moses Mendelssohn made such progress that by the time he was thirteen he was reading Moses Maimonides' *Guide to the Perplexed*, and he was fascinated by the work of the Jewish philosopher who had been born nearly six hundred years before him. As he studied the problems with which Maimonides had dealt in the twelfth century he realized that many fresh problems had arisen since then: some of these problems he was to resolve himself.

As a boy, he saw the problems but not the answers. He never tired of reading and study and he certainly overworked. When he started to grow a little—and he remained very small—it became clear not only that he would always be delicate but that he would also be hunchbacked; and he was further handicapped by a stutter. In after-life he would often refer jokingly to his deformity as a legacy from Moses Maimonides. "Maimonides spoilt my figure and ruined my digestion," he would say; "but still I dote on him, for although those long vigils with him weakened my body, they at the same time strengthened my soul: they stunted my stature, but they developed my mind."

Menachem Mendel had decided that his son should become a pedlar of small goods and carry his stock in a pack on his back. Many thirteen-year-old Jewish boys were already helping their families by peddling. But Moses, happy with his books, was bent on becoming a scholar like his teacher; and so his fond father let him continue his studies despite the poverty in which he and his wife were living.

Only a year after Mendel made this decision—in 1743—Rabbi Frankel was appointed Chief Rabbi of Berlin. This was a bitter blow to his pupil. It is said that the boy, tears streaming down his face, stood on a hillock by the roadside to say a last farewell to his master. When Frankel saw the weeping figure he took the boy in his arms and tried to comfort him with the hope that one day he, too, might go to Berlin.

Rabbi Frankel and Berlin now became the boy's goal. Six months later, having won the worried consent of his parents, he set out to walk the thirty miles from Dessau. The journey took him five days; and on the evening of the fifth he knocked wearily on the Jews' Gate of Berlin. When the watchman saw the miserable little figure he refused to let him in; for it was his duty to prevent vagrants from entering the city without means of support. Fortunately Moses had the presence of mind to stammer out that he was known to the Chief Rabbi and had come to join his classes; and so, reluctantly, the watchman opened the gate.

Touched by the boy's courage and devotion, Rabbi Frankel did what he could for him. He himself provided dinner on Sabbaths and festivals; and he persuaded another kind-hearted Jew to let Moses sleep in an attic in his house and give him a few meals during the week. He also found him work as a copyist; but the work was very poorly paid and the boy often went hungry. When he bought a loaf of bread Moses would notch it into sections, forcing himself not to eat more than one section in a day.

Like Hillel of old, Moses Mendelssohn barely noticed hunger or cold. Study took the place of food and warmth; and, with the determination born of enthusiasm, he continued to work on the *Talmud* under Rabbi Frankel. He also began to learn mathematics, French, English, Latin and Greek. From his tiny earnings he saved enough money to buy books, and he found several young teachers who were good enough to give him some help. There was one other subject that Moses Mendelssohn set himself to master: this was German. The Jews of the ghetto had lived all their lives in Germany, but since they were not allowed to mix with the Germans they had never learned to speak the language properly. Instead, they spoke Yiddish, a dialect of their own, which was a mixture of Hebrew and German.

Moses Mendelssohn began to learn German because he wanted to be able to speak it and to read German literature. Later on, he had another and more important reason. This was to try and draw Jews and Germans together. If, he thought, the language barrier could be removed the Germans would see that the despised Jews were in reality worthy of respect; and the Jews, in their turn, would lose their fear of the Germans. In this way friendship might in the end replace hatred.

After seven years of hard work and poor living Moses Mendelssohn was given the post of tutor to the children of a Jewish manufacturer of silk. The manufacturer, who was kind and sympathetic, allowed the young tutor ample time for his own studies. At the end of four years he made him book-keeper in his firm; and as time went on promoted him from one post to another until in the end he made him his partner. Mendelssohn took his business duties seriously; but his main interest was still study. As soon as he had gained enough background knowledge he plunged excitedly into the study of philosophy; and this new study became his chief interest.

Most of the intellectual young Jews of Berlin studied philosophy; and it was among them that Mendelssohn found most of his friends. They used to meet regularly to talk and play chess; and they formed a little community of their own. In 1749, however, a young German critic and writer named Gotthold Ephraim Lessing came to Berlin. Although he was only twenty (the same age as Mendelssohn), he had had one play accepted already. But he had lost his money by backing a theatrical company which failed; and in Berlin he worked hard as a journalist and translator. Lessing was extremely broadminded and loathed all forms of intolerance; and he showed his broadmindedness by accepting the young Jewish philosophers as equals and friends. Between Lessing and Mendelssohn in particular there grew up a warm and enduring friendship.

One of Lessing's earliest plays was called *The Jews*. In it he showed that, despised and outcast as they were, the Jews could be as generous and unselfish as anyone else. Needless to say, this play was not popular with the German authorities; but thirty years later, risking the spite and the anger which he knew it would arouse, Lessing wrote his drama, *Nathan the Wise*. This play, set at the time of the Third Crusade, tells of Nathan, a noble Jew, whose wife and children have been slaughtered by the Crusaders, but who yet finds it in his heart to adopt an orphaned Christian child and bring her up with affection and care. The rest of the drama (too long and complicated to describe here) shows Christian and Moslem alike won over by Nathan's simple goodness, his wisdom and tolerance, until Sultan Saladin himself admits that the Jews have much to teach the world.

For the character of Nathan, Moses Mendelssohn had served Lessing as a model. Friendship with the dramatist had drawn Mendelssohn into a much wider circle of literary men, for the Jew's knowledge of German made it possible for him to meet and make friends with Christians who shared

Lessing's tolerant ideas. At first Mendelssohn was very shy and awkward. His stunted figure and his stutter were against him: but he was so charming and witty, so enthusiastic and intelligent, that people soon forgot about his appearance.

Lessing also encouraged Mendelssohn to write in German on philosophical and literary topics; and the results were so good that they attracted a great deal of attention among the scholars of the day. It was clear that Mendelssohn was an exceedingly gifted writer; and as a result he joined with Lessing in founding a literary journal which soon became very well known.

In one issue of the journal Mendelssohn reviewed a volume of verse written in French by the King of Prussia, Frederick II—known as Frederick the Great. Mendelssohn thought the verse was poor and did not hesitate to say so; and he also disliked the habit, which was common among German writers at the time, of using French instead of German. It soon became public knowledge that a Jew had presumed to criticize the work of a king. A shocked courtier accused Mendelssohn of having "thrown aside all reverence for the most sacred person of His Majesty in insolent criticism of his poetry." Mendelssohn was commanded to appear at the royal palace in Potsdam and explain his conduct to the King. It was only his ready wit which saved him from serious trouble. "A maker of verses," he told the irritated Frederick, "plays at ninepins; and one who plays at ninepins, be he king or peasant, must abide by the decision of the marker on the result of his bowling." Grudgingly, Frederick agreed that, as a critic, Mendelssohn had been justified; but he never forgave him.

It was probably because of his criticism that the King denied him for a long time the privilege of becoming a "protected Jew." Under the existing rules Mendelssohn, who had not been born in the kingdom of Prussia, could live there only under the so-called protection of a Prussian-born Jew. The King could, if he wished, grant him the rare privilege of becoming a "protected Jew," which would mean that he could leave the ghetto and live in any part of Berlin he chose.

Some of his friends had drawn up a petition to secure the coveted title for Mendelssohn. At first he refused to allow it to go forward. He had no wish to beg for rights which should belong to every citizen; and he did not think that he should be singled out for a privilege which was denied to the majority of his fellow-Jews. At length he agreed that the petition might be presented; but only after his friends had persuaded him that for the sake of his family he ought not to refuse. The King had his revenge by accepting the petition but making Moses Mendelssohn wait an unreasonably long time before granting him the privilege.

When Mendelssohn was thirty-two he had married. He had fallen in love at first sight with a blue-eyed girl named Fromet (a name derived from the word *fromm*, meaning "pious"). Although her father was most anxious for the marriage to take place, Fromet was deterred by her suitor's appearance. "Is it she who objects?" he asked the father jokingly. "Then it must be my hump." He did not despair but waited until the girl had learned to know him. Before very long she changed her mind and the marriage took place. It was a very happy one; and in due course the Mendelssohns had several sons and daughters.

They began married life in a small house, uncomfortably crowded with twenty life-size china apes. Mendelssohn had not chosen the china apes, nor had they been given him as presents. In order to tax the Jews of Prussia as heavily as possible, a regulation was in force under which every Jewish bridegroom had to buy a large quantity of china from the King's manufactory. He was not allowed to select his own china but had to take whatever the makers wished to sell. But despite the lack of space, Mendelssohn's house became the meeting place of distinguished scholars and writers. Visitors to Berlin were anxious to meet the little hunchback, who had made a name for himself as a philosopher and a writer in German, yet remained a pious Jew. One of his visitors told a friend afterwards that on a dark Friday afternoon in winter he had turned to make some remark to his host, only to find that Moses Mendelssohn and his wife had quietly left the room. The door was open; and host and hostess could be seen in an adjoining room in the glow of the newly lit Sabbath candles. Deeply impressed by the simple ceremony, the guests rose to stand for a minute in respectful silence.

By now Mendelssohn was a famous man and, despite the fact that he was a Jew, he had many distinctions conferred on him. The Royal Academy of Sciences of Berlin had offered a prize for a learned essay on a most complex subject and Mendelssohn had decided to enter. But when he heard that some of the most brilliant scholars of the day were competing, including the scientist and philosopher Immanuel Kant, he nearly withdrew his own effort, so sure was he that it would fall far short of theirs. Yet it was Mendelssohn's essay which won the prize and won him great renown as well. He became still more famous with a philosophical book called *Phaedon, or the Immortality of the Soul*. The book was written in German in the form of the dialogue which had been made famous by the ancient Greek philosopher Plato; and in it Mendelssohn put forward all the arguments in support of a belief in immortality which religion, experience and reason have taught. *Phaedon* was widely read in Germany and translated into a number of languages, Hebrew among them. It gained for Moses Mendelssohn the highest recognition to which a German writer could aspire, an invitation to become a member of the Royal Academy. Owing to prejudice against him, Mendelssohn was unable to accept. The Empress of Russia, Catherine the Great, had apparently also been invited to join the Academy; and King Frederick, who thought she might be offended to discover that her fellow-member was a Jew, refused to give his consent to Mendelssohn's appointment.

The popularity of his book brought Mendelssohn into trouble. One of its admirers was a Swiss pastor and writer named Johann Lavater. In his zeal Lavater had dedicated to Mendelssohn a translation which he had made of a French book, *The Evidences of Christianity*; in the dedication he called on Mendelssohn to read his translation with an open mind, and then, if he felt he could refute the evidence of Christianity, to do so publicly: if, on the other hand, he was convinced of its truth, to accept conversion.

Lavater's request placed Mendelssohn in the most awkward predicament. He hated to see bad feelings aroused, especially religious feelings; and he had always refused to be drawn into an argument on the rival merits of Judaism and Christianity. But Lavater's dedication had been published, and he could not refuse to answer the challenge. First of all he stated with the utmost clarity that his faith in Judaism was unshakable. "Certain inquiries we finish once for all in our lives," he said. "And I herewith declare in the presence of the God of Truth, your and my Creator, by whom you have conjured me in your dedication, that I will adhere to my principles so long as my entire soul does not assume another nature." Nevertheless, it was useless to quarrel over religion; for those people who disliked and criticized the Jews would never be able to see any good in them as a result of a quarrel: their criticisms would only be silenced when they realized that they could respect the Jews for their qualities of character. "The contemptible opinion held of Jews," he declared, "I would desire to shame by virtue, not by controversy. My religion, my philosophy, and my standing in civil life are the weightiest arguments for avoiding all religious discussion." Judaism never sought converts from other religions; and, in return, he felt that no attempts should be made to convert the Jews. "I am so fortunate to count among my friends many a worthy man who is not of my faith," he went on. "Never yet has my heart whispered, 'Alas for this good man's soul!'"

Wisely, he refused to make any detailed criticism of *The Evidences of Christianity*. He made it quite clear that they could easily be refuted; but "Jews should be scrupulous in abstaining from reflections on the predominant religion." And, finally, he said that the book in no way altered his own allegiance to his faith.

The courtesy and restraint of Mendelssohn's reply brought an immediate and humble apology from Lavater. But other writers now intervened; and for nearly two years the sensitive Moses Mendelssohn was distressed by the articles, pamphlets and letters they wrote. In the end his critics were silenced by an unsigned pamphlet addressed to "those who wished to make Herr Moses Mendelssohn a Christian outright, or at least were genuinely surprised that he was not one already." The anonymous author scoffed at the idea that Mendelssohn could be converted to Christianity; and with the publication of his pamphlet the unhappy dispute died down.

Yet prejudice against the Jews seemed as strong as ever, as Mendelssohn's family knew only too well. When his sons and daughters were children he and his wife would take them for an evening walk in the streets of Berlin. Wherever they went they would be followed by boys who jeered and threw stones at them. "What have we done to them?" his children would ask pathetically. "Father, is it *wicked* to be a Jew?"

By his personal example and by active work Moses Mendelssohn was fighting against this senseless prejudice. The Jews of Switzerland, for example, faced with the prospect of harsh new restrictions on their liberty and opportunity, wrote to Mendelssohn begging him to take up their case with Pastor Lavater. This he did, although he might well have refused to have anything more to do with a man who had caused him so much unpleasantness; and Lavater was able to do something to lighten the new laws. A year or so later the Jews of Dresden learned that they were to be expelled because they could not pay the outrageously heavy taxes levied upon them. In their distress they turned to Moses Mendelssohn. He approached an acquaintance, an influential member of the privy council, who saw to it that this particular injustice was put right. Then the Jews of Alsace, shorn of all privileges and taxed beyond the limit, asked for Mendelssohn's help. This time he enlisted the aid of a Christian friend, an historian named Christian Wilhelm Dohm; for he was sure that the intervention of a Christian would have more chance of success than the intervention of a Jew. Dohm, a fearless man and a great admirer of Mendelssohn, decided to write something appealing for justice not for the Jews of Alsace alone but for all oppressed Jews. His work described the history and culture of the Jews of Europe and the cruel sufferings they had endured; and it claimed for them equal rights with other citizens; freedom to choose their occupation; and freedom to worship in their own way.

Dohm's action, in defiance of intolerance, was most courageous. His pamphlet was bitterly attacked and there were renewed outbreaks of anti-Jewish feeling. Yet very soon after its publication the Emperor of Austria issued decrees which gave the Jews rights they had never had before. Mendelssohn himself, anxious to reduce the ill-feeling, arranged for a translation into German to be made of Menasseh ben Israel's *Vindiciae Judaeorum*; and himself wrote a preface pleading for justice and tolerance. He also wrote another work, which he called *Jerusalem, or, Religious Power and Judaism*. In it he argued religious freedom; and exhorted his fellow Jews to cling loyally to their faith, despite prejudices against it.

When the French statesman Mirabeau, one of the first leaders of the French Revolution, read *Jerusalem* he was so impressed that he said he would like to see it translated into all European languages. The leaders of the Revolution, with their cry of "Liberty, Equality, Fraternity," were ready to grant equal privileges to all citizens of France, even to the Jews; and in 1790 the French Jews officially became citizens of the country of their birth.

Although France was the first country to recognize the Jews as equal citizens, the idea of equality had already been accepted in the newly-born United States of America. The first Jews to reach America had been refugees to New Amsterdam (as New York, then under Dutch rule, was called). By the middle of the eighteenth century Jews were scattered thinly over Britain's American colonies; and in the War of Independence about half of them sided with their new country. In the American colonies, as in England, the Jews had had to endure few restrictions. But when these colonies broke away to form the United States of America it was stipulated by the Constitution that for appointments to public office and other posts of trust there should be no religious barrier. There was not yet complete equality of citizenship. This was granted to the Jews in the various states at different times; and it was not until 1868 that the last of them, North Carolina, removed the few small restrictions which remained. From this date onwards the Jewish population rose very rapidly, fed by a stream of fugitives from Eastern Europe.

Meanwhile, in the countries overrun by Napoleon, as in France, the Jews had been granted equal rights. The freedom which Jews at last enjoyed put an end to the restricted life of the ghetto. Jews could mingle freely with Christians. Some decided, now that they were free to choose, to abandon their faith and adopt Christianity: and, while the majority remained staunch, there were marriages between Jews and Christians, and children were baptised into the Christian faith.

When at length the restrictions were removed in Germany a great deal of this kind of absorption occurred. Among the Jews who became Christians were the children of Moses Mendelssohn; although this did not happen during their father's lifetime.

During the last years of his life Mendelssohn had prepared the way for his people to mix socially with the Germans; but he would certainly not have approved of conversion. As we have seen, he wanted the Jews to learn the German language and to read German books; and so he decided to begin by giving them a translation into German of something which they knew and loved—the Pentateuch, the Five Books of Moses. He therefore translated the Pentateuch into German; and followed this with a translation of the Psalms. Young Jews who learned to read German from Mendelssohn's translations were quick to master the language and to turn to the literature. Before very long they had formed themselves into a band of German-Jewish writers; and they wrote not in the Yiddish dialect of their childhood but in German.

Mendelssohn also founded a school in which modern languages and technical subjects were taught in addition to the study of the *Talmud*. In these and other ways he was able to allay the fear and suspicion which the ghetto-born Jews felt for anything German.

And then, with many plans unrealized, Moses Mendelssohn died. He was only fifty-seven; but he had always been frail and had never spared himself. After his death Christians joined with Jews in mourning a great man and a great friend; for the delicate little hunchback born in the Dessau ghetto had proved himself one of the finest friends and staunchest leaders in the history of his people.

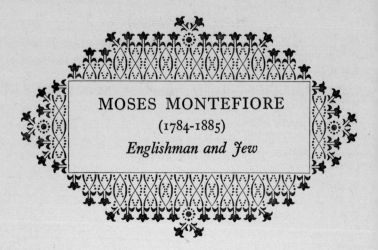

MOSES MONTEFIORE
(1784-1885)
Englishman and Jew

WHEN the life of Moses Montefiore, a loyal Jew and a loyal Englishman, opened in 1784, Jews and Christians who were not members of the Church of England —that is to say, Roman Catholics and Nonconformists— were not allowed to follow certain occupations. When his life ended at the very old age of 101, the last restrictions had long since been swept away.

Until the beginning of the nineteenth century British Jews could not hold any public office; they could not enter Parliament or the universities; they could not take part in local government, or become lawyers; and their children might not attend non-Jewish schools. Because so many professions were forbidden them and in others only a small number were accepted, Jews turned to the professions from which they were not barred: they became merchants; they entered commerce, finance or banking. The restrictions against the Jews of England were very slight compared with those in other parts of Europe. In England, Jews could live where they chose; engage in any business or branch of manufacture; and employ non-Jewish workmen. But Jews—together with Catholics and Noncomformists—were not completely free and equal citizens of their country.

The family of Moses Montefiore, which may originally

have come from Spain or Portugal, had settled in Italy early in the seventeenth century. Their name was probably taken from an Italian village (there were at least two villages in Italy called Montefiore). Jews were by this time obliged to use surnames instead of calling themselves the sons of their father (like Menasseh ben Israel or Moses Mendelssohn). They had to do this to make it easier for tax collectors to keep records of the money paid by Jews in taxes; and so many Jews adopted place names.

In the early part of the eighteenth century the Montefiore family left Italy for England and settled in Kennington in London. Moses was the eldest of the family of three sons and five daughters of Joseph Elias Montefiore and his wife Rachel, who belonged to the Mocatta family, one of the first Spanish-Jewish families to leave Spain.

The Montefiore boys went to a local school and they were taught Hebrew by one of their uncles. Their schooldays ended when they were still very young, and Moses was sent to learn the grocery business in the City of London under a Christian friend of his parents. He was not interested in the business and did not want to make it his life's work. A number of his relatives had become successful financiers, and some had joined the London Stock Exchange. He decided that he, too, would like to be a stockbroker; but this was not easy. At the time the number of Jewish stockbrokers on the Stock Exchange was limited to twelve; and a large sum of money was needed to pay for the privilege of becoming a member. But Moses, an exceedingly tall and goodlooking young man, with sincerity of purpose and a most charming manner, was much liked by his wealthy relations; and when a vacancy on the Stock Exchange occurred, they bought it for him.

Moses Montefiore was such a successful stockbroker that by the time he was forty he had made a fortune and was able to retire. In the meantime, in 1812, he had married Judith Cohen, whose father, also a wealthy man, had come to England from Holland as a young man. The marriage was a very happy one, but there were no children. The fact that Moses and Judith Montefiore were childless drew them closer together; and in the important work which Moses undertook after his retirement his wife was constantly with him.

The marriage also linked the two branches of Jewry, known as the Sephardim and the Ashkenazim. The Sephardim (identified with the Biblical Sephared) came originally from Spain and Portugal. The Ashkenazim (according to tradition Ashkenaz was a great-grandson of Noah) came from Germany and Poland. As we have seen, the first Jews to enter Holland, and the first to re-enter England, came from Spain and Portugal. These Sephardi Jews were very different from the German and Polish fugitives who also flocked to Holland. The Sephardim kept aloof from the Ashkenazim, who had lived in ghettoes and were so much less cultured and polished. One difference between them was that while Spanish and Portuguese Jews had been forced to follow their faith in secret and in constant danger, the ghetto Jews, ill-treated and oppressed as they had been, had never had to conceal their religion. There were other differences as well. The Sephardim and the Ashkenazim spoke different languages and pronounced Hebrew differently. Their customs and their ways were different: they worshipped in separate synagogues with separate prayer-books and with separate spiritual leaders: they sent their children to different schools: and each community supported its own charities. In fact, they had as little to do with one another as possible; and while the Sephardim were inclined to look down on the newcomers, the Ashkenazim considered the Sephardim unbearably superior.

So when Moses Montefiore, a Sephardi Jew, married Judith Cohen, an Ashkenazi, he was doing something to bridge the gap which at that time existed between the two branches of Anglo-Jewry. Both branches benefited; for when Montefiore retired from the Stock Exchange he devoted all his time and a great deal of his fortune to charitable causes; and he was generous to the Ashkenazi community as well as to the Sephardi. More than this, he took part in the running of several Ashkenazi concerns—a training college for ministers, a school and a hospital.

After Montefiore retired he still kept up his interest in the City. He helped, among other activities, to found the Alliance Assurance Company, because Jews seemed to have difficulty in persuading other companies to accept them for fire and other forms of insurance; and to this day his portrait hangs in the place of honour over the fireplace in the Company's boardroom. He also helped to found the Gas Company which provided gas lighting in various continental cities; and his work for this Company was one of the reasons why the Royal Society, the oldest and most famous scientific body in Britain, honoured him by appointing him a Fellow. His most important act was to join with his brother-in-law, the famous financier Nathan Mayer Rothschild, in arranging a loan of £20,000,000 to the British Government. This was in 1833, the year in which Britain, the first country to put an end to the slave-trade (the inhuman buying and selling of African men, women and children), decreed that all the slaves still living in her dominions should be set free. The money was used by the British Government to compensate the slave-owners for the loss of their slaves; for as soon as the slaves were freed they had to be paid wages for work which they had previously been forced to do for nothing.

Not long after his retirement Moses Montefiore and his wife moved from Kennington to a fashionable part of London, Park Lane, and they lived there for the rest of their lives. Montefiore was always extremely busy. For many years he had served the Jewish community and also the country as a whole. He had, for example, been an officer in the Surrey Regiment of Volunteers, a regiment which had been raised during the Napoleonic Wars at a time when Britain feared a French invasion. In the Sephardi community he held high office and spent day after day arranging help for the needy. He attended synagogue services regularly and observed all the laws of his religion. On the Sabbath he would often walk long distances to visit somebody who needed his help; and when he went abroad he would eat no meat. In the course of his long life he attended many public banquets, and he was careful to observe the dietary laws. "Took my own cold beef," he wrote in his diary after attending a dinner in aid of a non-Jewish charity.

There seemed no end to Montefiore's generosity, for he loved to give. The first of many large benefactions was the gift of thirteen houses for needy members of the Sephardi community. But his chief work outside his own synagogue was for the Jewish Board of Deputies, the body which had been set up to represent Jewish interests. When Montefiore joined the Board it was working for the repeal of the restrictions against Jews. He was appointed a member of the committee whose job it was to find out what, if anything, the Government was prepared to do; and he was in the centre of activities when one by one the restrictions were removed. Within a few years of joining the Board of Deputies Montefiore was made President; and with one or two intervals, when he was abroad on special missions, he held the office until he was a very old man.

Soon after he joined the Board of Deputies, Montefiore bought a large house and gardens with adjoining land at the seaside town of Ramsgate in Kent. East Cliff Lodge, as it was called, stood on a high cliff; and it possessed two subterranean passages leading down to the seashore, which were thought to have been made by smugglers.

East Cliff Lodge became the Montefiores' best-loved home. After buying the house Montefiore's first thought was to build a synagogue. On a Saturday evening in August, 1831, when the Sabbath was over, Montefiore and his wife, with members of his family and friends, went to the site which he had chosen and placed two bricks to form the beginning of the wall at the back of the Ark. Next morning the foundation stones were laid and sprinkled with earth which Montefiore had brought back from a recent visit to Palestine. The synagogue took nearly two years to complete. When it was ready a large congregation attended the solemn service of dedication. But the day ended with celebrations of a different kind—a banquet, a dance, and fireworks.

For the upkeep of the synagogue Montefiore had set aside a special fund. But his generosity was not confined to his

own religion and people. The Christian clergymen of Ramsgate could always count on his help in their charitable causes;
and he made a habit of giving each of them a certain sum of
money to spend as he thought fit.

As the owner of East Cliff Lodge Montefiore became one
of the leading citizens of the town; and his importance was
recognized later when he was appointed High Sheriff for the
county of Kent and Deputy Lieutenant—the Queen's commissioner for the county. In 1835 the Duchess of Kent and
her sixteen-year-old daughter, Princess Victoria, visited Ramsgate, and Montefiore was invited to lead a deputation of
welcome. The sheltered gardens of his house were thrown
open to the royal visitors, and Montefiore presented the
Duchess with a key wrapped in rich blue ribbon. Afterwards the Duchess and her daughter stayed for some
time in the district, and Montefiore had a special gate made
in the wall so that they could go in and out of the gardens
freely.

They never forgot his kindness. In the autumn of 1836
he received an invitation to dinner. "I attended Synagogue,"
he wrote in his diary, "and a little before seven went in our
chariot to West Cliff, where I had the honour of dining with
their Royal Highnesses. . . . There were thirteen at table, and
it was impossible for it to have been more agreeable. I never
felt myself more at ease at any dinner party within my re-
collection."

A few months after the dinner party Montefiore was
elected to an office of the Crown, as Sheriff of London. Two
years earlier the work of the Board of Deputies had led to the
passing of an Act of Parliament which made it possible for a
Jew to hold this office. Two Sheriffs for London were
elected yearly (as they are elected today) by a court presided
over by the Lord Mayor. The first Jew to become a Sheriff
was David Salomons, a nephew-in-law of Judith Montefiore;
and Moses Montefiore was the second.

The date of his inauguration fell on a Jewish festival. "The
day I enter on my office," he wrote, "is the commencement of
our New Year. I shall therefore have to walk to Westminster

instead of going in my state carriage, nor, I fear, shall I be able to dine with my friends at the inauguration dinner." In deference to Montefiore's observance of the New Year the date of the inauguration was changed, and he was able to take full part in the ceremonies.

In the same year, 1837, he became the first Jew to be elected a Fellow of the Royal Society. 1837 was the year in which Princess Victoria became Queen; and Montefiore was a member of several deputations of congratulations, one from the Board of Deputies, one from the Borough of Ramsgate, and a third from the City Companies of London. When the eighteen-year-old Queen Victoria entered the City on Lord Mayor's Day, November 9th, she conferred the honour of knighthood on him. "On my kneeling to the Queen," he wrote, "she placed a sword on my left shoulder and said, 'Rise, Sir Moses.' I cannot express all I felt on this occasion. I had, besides, the pleasure of seeing my banner with 'Jerusalem' floating proudly in the hall." (The word 'Jerusalem' in Hebrew characters was inscribed on the escutcheon of the Montefiore arms.)

Jerusalem was very much more to Sir Moses than a name on his escutcheon. He and his wife had been to Palestine (which was part of the Turkish Empire) ten years earlier, and this was the first of a number of visits. On their original visit the Montefiores had stayed only a few days in Jerusalem; but it was long enough for them to see how poverty-stricken were the Jews there, and how little effort they made to better their conditions. They seemed content to exist on charity from the Jews of other countries and they spent their days in prayer and religious study. About 650 Jews lived in Jerusalem: the rest of the small Jewish population lived in the cities of Hebron, Tiberias (founded by Joseph Nasi), and Safed. There was no time during this visit to do anything to improve their conditions; but it was clear to Montefiore that what they needed most was to learn how to help themselves. On his way, however, Montefiore had had an audience with Mehemet Ali, the Viceroy of Egypt, who later, under the Sultan of Turkey, became the ruler of Egypt and also, for a time, of Syria and Palestine. The audience had important results in the future.

The Montefiores' second visit to Palestine was in the late autumn of 1838. The journey across Europe in those days was a slow one by horse-drawn coach or carriage. It was a difficult one, too, and not without danger, for mountain roads were often flooded or covered in ice and snow. "My dear Judith," wrote Sir Moses, "was often so frightened that she persisted in getting out of the carriage although the snow was deep on the ground. Our courier and the postillions had to walk a great part of the way, and to lead the horses, as the ice had made the roads so slippery."

Judith Montefiore was a woman of courage. She was not very strong, and a bad fall in childhood had left her slightly deformed; but she would not allow her health to prevent her from going with her "dear Monte" (as she called her husband) wherever he went. She was also a woman of intelligence, who spoke several languages fluently and was a student of Hebrew and Arabic; and she supported her husband in all his schemes.

Sir Moses had come to Palestine with the object of helping the poverty-stricken Jews; and wherever he went he gave money gifts not to the Jews alone but to needy Christians and Moslems as well. But the giving of money, which could only be of temporary help, was not his real object. His plan was to obtain from Mehemet Ali a grant of land which could be cultivated by the Jews of Palestine and by Jews from other countries who wished to settle in the Holy Land. The money to buy the land would be raised by a colonization company, which would also make arrangements for new settlers. Montefiore saw Mehemet Ali again on his way home and described his plan. He received a vague answer; and nothing more came of it at the time, for soon afterwards Mehemet Ali was driven out of Palestine and Syria and kept his authority only in Egypt.

In the meantime an event had taken place in Syria which had placed the Jewish inhabitants in grave peril. A monk of Damascus, Father Tommaso, had disappeared without a trace; and the Jews of Damascus were accused of murdering him for ritual purposes. The leaders of the Jewish community were arrested and tortured in a vain attempt to extract a confession of guilt. Some died under torture. The survivors were condemned to die, but sentence of death could not be carried out until confirmed by Mehemet Ali. When news of the false accusation and its dreadful consequences reached Europe, the Jews were deeply distressed and highly indignant. In England, Christians as well as Jews were angry; and a meeting of protest was held in London presided over by the Lord Mayor. The Jewish communities of England and France then decided to send a small party of distinguished Jews to Egypt to try and secure justice for the men under sentence of death. On the way back they were asked to visit Constantinople to refute a second charge of ritual murder which had been made against the Jews of the island of Rhodes, another part of the Turkish Empire. The chief French representative of the party was a statesman and lawyer, Isaac Crémieux: the chief British representative was Sir Moses Montefiore. Before he left England, Sir Moses was received in audience by the Queen. He was also given letters of recommendation by the Foreign Office to show that he went not simply as the representative of British Jews but as the representative of the British Government. Crémieux did not receive the same support from the French Government; and the French consul at Damascus, despite all the evidence, was convinced that the Jews were guilty.

The mission arrived in Alexandria to find Egypt in a state of unrest. But despite a crisis in foreign affairs Sir Moses gained an audience with his old acquaintance Mehemet Ali and asked him for permission to go to Damascus and establish the innocence of the prisoners on the spot. Mehemet Ali refused; but Sir Moses called on the European consuls to ask for their support. All, save the French consul, agreed. A general request was therefore sent to Mehemet Ali demanding the release of the prisoners. Somewhat alarmed, he agreed, and gave the imprisoned Jews what he called an "honourable liberation."

As Mehemet Ali was no longer as powerful as he had been, the mission decided to go on to Constantinople and get the order confirmed by his overlord, the Sultan of Turkey. The Sultan received Sir Moses with great courtesy. He gave an undertaking that he would protect his Jewish subjects; and he promptly issued a decree declaring that the accusations of ritual murder which had been made against the Jews of Damascus and Rhodes were absolutely false. "We cannot," he declared, "permit the Jewish nation (whose innocence of the crime alleged against them is evident) to be vexed and tormented upon accusations which have not the least foundation in truth." And he promised that the Jews should "possess the same advantages and enjoy the same privileges as are granted to the numerous other nations who submit to our authority."

The innocence of the Jews had been clearly established; and those who had survived torture and imprisonment were released. One thing Sir Moses had been unable to achieve. This was the removal of a memorial tablet in Damascus to Father Tommaso, which stated that he had been assassinated by the Jews. The tablet remained in place until the church which housed it was destroyed by fire some years later.

Sir Moses returned to London bringing with him a copy of the Sultan's decree which he presented to the Queen. In recognition of what he had done the Queen granted him a special mark of her esteem, the addition of supporters— the representation of figures supporting the escutcheon on the Montefiore arms. The supporters were added for Montefiore's "unceasing exertions on behalf of his injured and persecuted brethren in the East and the Jewish nation at large." Messages and addresses of gratitude reached Sir Moses from all over Europe, and he was congratulated by many Christians as well as Jews. He accepted the congratulations and the royal goodwill very humbly. "The supporters I wish for," he wrote in his diary, "are to exalt our holy religion by displaying 'Jerusalem' in a more distinguished manner than I could otherwise have done."

The success of this first mission led to others. The next

mission Sir Moses undertook was to Russia. For many years, as we saw, Poland was the most important home of Jewish life. But in the last years of the eighteenth century Poland was in a state of chaos and, as a result, nearby Russia stepped in and annexed a large part of Polish territory. Over a million Jews lived in this territory, and at first the Russians did not know what to do with them. They wanted to make them more Russian and less Jewish, and so after a time they introduced a harsh form of military conscription. Jewish boys were rounded up and forced to serve in the army for a period of twenty-five years. Another edict was issued, ordering the removal to the interior of nearly a hundred thousand Jews who lived on the frontiers of Russia bordering those of Germany and Austria. It was a cruel hardship for these Jews to leave their homes, and they appealed to Sir Moses for help. At the same time as he received the appeal, Sir Moses learned that the Emperor of Russia, the Czar Nicholas I, would like to consult him about some form of education for his Jewish subjects.

Accompanied by his wife, Sir Moses led a deputation to Russia in the spring of 1846. The journey across Europe took a month, and the icy Russian spring made the going dangerous. On April 8th Nicholas I, supreme ruler of Russia, received Sir Moses in audience. "Praised be the God of our Fathers," wrote Sir Moses afterwards, "at one o'clock this day I had the honour of an interview with his Imperial Majesty the Emperor. I made the strongest appeal in my power for the general alteration of all laws and edicts that pressed heavily on the Jews under his Majesty's sway." In reply, the Czar said that he would do something for his Jewish subjects; and he suggested that Montefiore should visit the various Jewish communities and talk over the problems with Russian officials and Jews. This he did. Everywhere he went Sir Moses was greeted with deference by the Russian authorities and with overwhelming affection and pride by the Jews. He gained a good deal of useful information and submitted his views to the Czar's ministers. As a result, Nicholas, who had been planning an even heavier programme of restrictions, abandoned his project.

The advice which Montefiore had given the Russian Jews was the advice that Moses Mendelssohn had given the Jews of Germany—to learn the language of their country and adopt its customs and way of life. In this manner, loyal both to their religion and their country, they would be ready for the rights and privileges of full citizenship which, he was sure, would be theirs in the end. The Jews listened with respect: but they felt threatened at every turn and so terrified of the future that they could not bring themselves to take his advice and clung more strongly than ever to their own traditions.

The return journey through Germany was like a royal procession. Wherever the Montefiores' carriage drew up it was surrounded by a crowd of German Jews eager to thank Sir Moses for the work he was doing, work which affected the welfare of the Jews of all Europe as well as the Jews of the East. On his arrival in London the Queen conferred a baronetcy on him in recognition of the unique position he held among his fellow-Jews and in order to encourage him to continue his much-needed work.

Sir Moses needed no encouragement. Appeals for help and advice now poured in on him from all over the East, from Palestine, Syria, Morocco, Persia and elsewhere; and to each appeal he gave his time and his service. His special concern was for the Jews of Palestine, and he visited the country three times between 1849 and 1857, distributing money to needy Jews and non-Jews. When, two years later, civil war broke out in the Lebanon, leaving many Christians destitute and starving, he organized an appeal to the British public to help them. In Palestine, he had been permitted by the Turkish authorities to buy a small piece of land on which the Montefiore suburb of Tel Aviv stands today: and he had also provided the money to found a school for Jewish girls. But this was not enough. He was still hoping to gain permission for the founding of a colonization company.

On one of his early visits to Palestine Montefiore was struck by the overcrowded conditions inside the walled city of Jerusalem; and he realized that if more Jews came to live in Jerusalem houses would be needed outside the walls. He therefore built some houses on high ground beyond the city, and offered them to Jews at very low rents. But no one would live in them, for fear that without the safety of the ancient walls they would be attacked by Moslem Arabs. Watchmen were then provided to guard the houses, but still the people hesitated until, in the end, they were actually paid to live there. When no harm came to them, more houses were built; and the buildings spread until they formed part of a modern city outside the old walled city—the New Jerusalem. In Montefiore's honour this part of the modern city is called *Yemin Moshe*—which means the right, or the right arm, of Moses.

Returning by way of Alexandria from his fifth visit to Palestine, Montefiore met Prince Said, a son of Mehemet Ali and afterwards Viceroy of Egypt. The Prince, who visited England some time afterwards, stayed with the Montefiores, and he liked them so much that when he decided to have his own son, Toussoun Pasha, educated in England, he asked the Montefiores to take care of the boy. Toussoun Pasha, a child of four or five, stayed with the Montefiores in London several times, and was presented by Sir Moses to the Queen.

In 1858, not long after the Montefiores returned from their fifth visit to Palestine, one of the chief barriers to Jewish equality in England was swept away: professing Jews were able to enter Parliament. It is true that Benjamin Disraeli (afterwards Lord Beaconsfield) was a leading figure in the House of Commons; but Disraeli, although a Jew by birth, had been baptised a Christian. The reason why professing Jews had been debarred from Parliament was that each Member had to take an oath of allegiance "on the faith of a Christian," holding in his hand a copy of the New Testament. In order to draw attention to this injustice, a nephew of Sir Moses, Baron Lionel de Rothschild, had on four separate occasions been elected to Parliament as a Member for the City of London. Each time he had refused to take the oath of allegiance in the prescribed form and had been unable to take his seat in the House. In 1858, however, an Act was passed giving both Houses of Parliament the right to decide on the form of oath administered to a Jew. The words "on the faith of a Christian" were struck out and Jews were no longer called on to swear on the New Testament. When, for the fifth time, Lionel de Rothschild was elected by the City of London, he became the first British Jew to take his seat in the House of Commons. His election was a source of pride to Sir Moses, who had worked ceaselessly for the removal of all restrictions against his people.

Montefiore was nearing eighty by now, an old man but upright and full of energy. In June, 1862, he and his wife celebrated their golden wedding; but it was clear to their relatives and friends that Lady Montefiore, who had been ill for some time, could not live long. Three months later, on the eve of the Jewish New Year, she lay in bed listening to the evening service which was held in a room of prayer near her bedroom. When the service was over Sir Moses came to give her his blessing, as he did each Sabbath and on every festival; and she replied by placing her hand for a moment on his head. He had scarcely left the room to join members of his family downstairs, when he was hurriedly recalled; and he was at his wife's bedside when she died a few minutes later. Lady Montefiore was buried at Ramsgate near the synagogue which she and her husband had built so many years before; and in the course of time he was buried in the same tomb. As a memorial to the wife he had loved so dearly Sir Moses built and endowed at Ramsgate a college for the training of ministers of religion. He himself lived on for more than twenty years, years in which he continued his work and used his great influence tirelessly on behalf of the oppressed Jews.

Sir Moses journeyed to Constantinople, where a new Sultan undertook to honour all the concessions and privileges which his father had granted to his Jewish subjects. He went to Morocco and gained the release of a number of Jews who had been imprisoned on a false charge of murdering a Spaniard. He also secured an undertaking from the Sultan of Morocco that in future Jews and Christians should have the same rights before the law as Moslems.

When he reached England once more he was given a tremendous welcome. No fewer than two thousand addresses of thanks reached him from Jews all over the world. In the City of London a public meeting of thanks was held, with his nephew, Alderman David Salomons, in the chair; and with Britain's future Prime Minister, William Ewart Gladstone, as one of the speakers. Meetings were also held in other parts of the country: and the crowning award accorded Sir Moses was the Freedom of the City of London, a tribute reserved for rulers and for men who have rendered the greatest service to their country. This tribute, said the Lord Mayor, was bestowed on him as a Jew and in recognition of his "wearisome journeys" to help his own people and also those of other creeds and denominations.

The "wearisome journeys" continued. In 1865 Sir Moses paid his sixth visit to Palestine—the first without his wife. He distributed money for relief of the distress caused by an outbreak of disease and famine; but he was still seeking a way to solve the old problems of poverty and want.

At the age of eighty-two he went to Rumania in answer to a piteous appeal from the Rumanian Jews who were suffering under a sudden wave of persecution. Sir Moses went as the representative of the Jewish Board of Deputies; but he was supported by the British Government and the Governments of Russia and Prussia; and also assured of support by the Emperor Napoleon III of France, who received him in Paris. In Bucharest, Sir Moses was met with promises of help by Prince Charles of Rumania. But his arrival in the city led to a renewed outbreak of persecution. An angry mob, incited by an article in an anti-Jewish newspaper, surrounded the hotel where Sir Moses and the other members of the deputation were staying. Without a thought for his own safety, Sir Moses appeared at an open window. "Fire away, if you like!" he cried. "I came here in the name of justice and humanity to plead the cause of innocent sufferers." Impressed by his courage the mob melted away; but an armed guard was stationed outside the building to protect him. Sir Moses refused to remain in the safety of the hotel, but insisted in driving through the streets of the city alone in an open carriage. "Everyone shall see me," he said when his friends tried to prevent him from going. "It is a holy cause; that of justice and humanity. I trust in God. He will protect me."

Sir Moses was not attacked during the drive; and later, when he left Bucharest, he was escorted by a cavalry guard of honour, as a mark of Prince Charles' esteem.

Not long after his return from his mission to Rumania the last of the restrictions against British Jews was removed. In 1871 an Act of Parliament was passed which enabled a Jew to hold any office of state. In the same year a Jew—Sir George Jessel—was appointed Solicitor-General, and thus became the first Jew to be made a minister of the Crown. From 1871 onwards the Jews of Britain have enjoyed absolute equality with their fellow-citizens.

A few years later, at the age of eighty-eight, Sir Moses Montefiore visited Russia for the second time. There was now a new Czar, Alexander II, a wise and enlightened ruler who had given his Jewish subjects a large measure of freedom. Sir Moses was overjoyed to find how much better the Jews were treated under Alexander than they had been on his first visit twenty-six years earlier. The reason for his mission was not on this occasion an appeal for help. He had come with congratulations to the Czar from the Board of Deputies on the two hundredth anniversary of the Emperor Peter the Great. The Czar was away on military exercises when Sir Moses reached the capital, St. Petersburg (now Leningrad); but when he learned that his aged guest had arrived he returned specially in order to spare Sir Moses the trouble of an extra journey.

Peace for the Jews of Russia was short-lived. Nine years later Alexander II, who had done so much to help his poorest subjects—serfs and peasants as well as Jews—was assassinated by revolutionaries. After his death the Jews were involved in a series of terrible massacres. Those who could afford it began to leave Russia in growing numbers and to find new homes for themselves in the freedom and security of Britain and the United States. Others longed only for Palestine, the Holy Land.

Sir Moses was ninety when he paid his seventh and final visit to Palestine. Christians and Moslems joined with Jews to make him welcome and show him what his help had meant to them. For the last time he spoke to the Jews of the need to work and support themselves and their families; and was pleased to find many of them eager and willing to do so. He was as anxious as ever for land to be bought and cultivated by all the Jews who wanted to make Palestine their home: and on his return to England, a Palestine Colonization Society was formed to devise means of putting his ideas into effect.

His days of active work were now at an end. Had he been strong enough, Sir Moses would have gone again, at the age of ninety-two, to Morocco to help his fellow-Jews, and to Russia to try and stem the wave of persecution which broke out after Alexander's assassination. But although he was too feeble to undertake another mission, Sir Moses could still write letters refuting false charges made against the Jews; and he could still help Jews and non-Jews with his money.

On his ninety-ninth birthday Sir Moses received a telegram of congratulations from Queen Victoria, on "entering the hundredth year of a useful and honourable life." And so many visitors came to Ramsgate to congratulate him personally that extra trains had to be run. Throughout Thanet— the area of Kent which contains Ramsgate and other seaside towns—the day was celebrated as a general holiday. Streets and ships were decorated, and after dark there were illuminations. But the greatest happiness which his ninety-ninth birthday brought Sir Moses was the knowledge that his hopes of cultivating land in Palestine for Jewish settlement were at last to be realized. A society called the "Lovers of Zion" had been formed for the purpose of settling Jews in the Holy Land; and during the next few months Sir Moses sent money to help six new Jewish farming settlements.

On his hundredth birthday, in 1884, Sir Moses received

another telegram from the Queen, and there were further celebrations. At Ramsgate there was a special service in his own synagogue; and because Sir Moses was too frail to attend, prayers were recited in his presence at East Cliff Lodge. A friend described him afterwards as he sat, wrapped in a purple silk dressing-gown, in the corner of a high-backed sofa supported by pillows, while sunshine "rested gently upon a grand head, full of character, fringed with a short, closely cut, snow-white beard."

Until the end of his life—and he was nearly a hundred and one when he died—Sir Moses retained his interest in Palestine and in the many schemes he had helped to launch; and to the very end his mind was clear and his enthusiasm unshaken. After his death people everywhere spoke of him as the finest representative of the Jewish people, a loyal Jew and a loyal Englishman. In the City of London, which he had served so faithfully, a meeting was called the day after his death, at which the Lord Mayor declared that "the most distinguished citizen of London" had passed away. And on this occasion it was also said of him most truly that he was leaving "behind him a memory which will be long cherished in many lands."

THEODOR HERZL
(1860-1904)
Builder of Zion

Among the many people who came to Ramsgate to congratulate Sir Moses Montefiore on his hundredth birthday were members of the newly formed society the Lovers of Zion; and, as we have seen, before he died Sir Moses sent money towards the upkeep of six farming settlements in Palestine. The first colonists of these settlements were students, who took as their watchword a quotation from the Book of Isaiah: "O house of Jacob, come ye, and let us go forth." Using the initial letters of this quotation in Hebrew, the students called themselves "Bilu": and in 1882 they had founded a settlement not very far from Jaffa called Rishon le-Zion, which means "First in Zion." In the following years Jews fleeing from persecution and death in Eastern Europe founded other settlements. These Jews were desperately poor. There were no houses for them to live in, and very little water: they knew nothing about farming; and the Bedouin—the wandering Arab tribes—were suspicious and hostile. The new settlements might well have failed but for the generosity of a wealthy French Jew, Baron Edmond de Rothschild, who for fifty years provided regular funds for the resettlement of Jews in Palestine.

But progress was very slow; and all the time, to more and more Jews Palestine was becoming a symbol of hope and refuge. In Western, as in Eastern Europe hatred was being stirred up against them. It started in Germany, encouraged by the powerful Minister of Foreign Affairs, Prince von Bismarck. Freed from the old life of the ghetto, Jews were showing intelligence and great ability in public life; and Bismarck feared their influence, especially in politics. He had nothing against the Jews as a people, but it suited his purpose that Germans should believe that the old false accusations against them were true, and also that they were plotting to overthrow the state. In this way the Jews were made into a scapegoat—or a victim—to be blamed for any troubles which beset Germany. The word which describes this unreasonable and unreasoning hatred of the Jews is "antisemitism."

The hatred whipped up in Germany quickly spread to nearby Austria and Hungary, which together formed an empire. It also extended to France; and it was fanned by the publication of violently antisemitic books written in German and French. The result was fear and loathing of the Jews both as a people and as individuals. If, for example, a German failed in business it was easy for him to claim that it was not his fault but the fault of the greedy, dishonest Jews who had forced him out of business. And his failure made him ready to believe that a Jewish conspiracy existed to deprive Christians of all the trade and business in the world.

The antisemitism which Bismarck encouraged in Germany in the early 1870s was to lead (as we shall see) to the most dreadful catastrophe of our own day. At first it was barely noticed by many of the Jews who had merged themselves successfully—or become assimilated—in the life of the country. A prosperous Jewish family named Herzl who lived in the Hungarian capital, Budapest, scarcely knew that it existed. The head of the family was Jacob Herzl, an honest and vigorous merchant. His wife, Jeannette, an exceedingly beautiful woman, with heavy black hair and fine features, was warmhearted and sincere. She was also extremely sensitive; and in conversation sparkling and witty. The Herzls had two children, a daughter, Pauline, born in 1859, and a son, Theodor, born the following year. Pauline was a beautiful child, very like her mother. Theodor, a handsome and striking-looking boy, resembled both his parents. He had his mother's large dark eyes under thick black eyebrows, and her sensitive rather sad expression; and his father's strong square-shaped head and his firm, full lips. From his mother Theodor inherited brilliance and wit and the tendency to sadness which sensitive people so often feel. From his father he inherited drive, determination and ability.

The Herzls were a united and devoted family and a great deal of love and attention was given to the children, who responded with affection for their parents and for one another. Theirs was the close family devotion which has been found through the years among Jews in all parts of the world, and which is often used as an example of the ideal family life.

Young Theodor was sent to his first school—a Jewish school—at the age of six. The teachers found him very intelligent and lively and also well-behaved. But he took little interest in the religious teaching at school, for the Bible stories were told in so dull and dry a way that he disliked having to listen to them.

The Herzls' house in Budapest was next door to a synagogue, and the family attended the services regularly. But they mixed so much with non-Jewish friends and people who lived nearby, and Mrs. Herzl was so much more interested in German than Jewish literature and culture, that the children grew up in the German rather than the Jewish tradition, and had no real feeling about their religion.

Even as a boy, however, Theodor experienced anti-semitism. His first idea was to become an engineer and so his parents took him away from his Jewish school and enrolled him at a technical school. He was already something of a writer and at the technical school he founded a literary society, with himself as president. His interest soon veered from scientific subjects to literature, and his engineering work suffered accordingly. At fifteen he left the school, partly because he showed so little aptitude for engineering; but also—as he said himself—because he was angered past all bearing by one of the teachers, who defined the meaning of the word "heathen" as "idolators, Mohammedans and Jews."

Theodor's next school was a high school, in which there were so many Jewish pupils that there was no antisemitism. He began to write seriously while still at school; and some of his poems, essays and reviews were published in a Hungarian newspaper.

Pauline, Theodor's sister and earliest friend, was as promising as her brother. She had her mother's love of literature; she was a fine pianist, and a brilliant amateur actress. She was gay, beautiful and extremely popular; and when she went to her first ball she danced through the night, radiant and lovely. But the next day she developed a heavy cold which soon turned to pneumonia. Within a few days, despite everything the doctors could do for her, Pauline was dead.

Stricken with grief, her parents could not bear to live in their old home any longer. As soon as Theodor had taken his university entrance examinations, they left Budapest for Vienna, the Austrian capital, taking their son with them. Theodor never really recovered from his sister's death. Theirs had been such a very close friendship, dating from early childhood when they used to walk about together hand in hand. When some years later his first daughter was born the baby was named Pauline. When he wrote a novel, the heroine was based on the character of his sister and the book was dedicated to her memory. And after her death the tendency to sadness which he inherited from his mother became more marked.

Pauline's death left Theodor the mainspring of his parents' life, his mother's one hope. The love and attention they lavished on him now was so great that in a sense he never outgrew it, as he never outgrew the loss of his sister. Although he was to marry and have children of his own, the marriage was not a very happy one; and he remained rather too wrapped up in his parents, especially in his mother. But, as people have said, if his marriage had been ideally happy he might never have felt the urge to lose himself in work for a cause: and the return of Jews to their ancient home in Palestine might have been delayed for an indefinite time.

Meanwhile, before he left Budapest Theodor had made up his mind to be a writer. But his anxious parents persuaded him that writing was not a full-time job; and so he agreed to study law at the University of Vienna. When he had graduated as a Doctor of Laws he built up a legal practice. He was exceedingly ambitious; and he knew that with his ability, his fine voice and his good looks he was capable of rising high in his profession. But he also knew that, as a Jew, he would be debarred from becoming a judge; and so, after a year, he threw up law and returned to his writing. He wrote easily and well, turning out articles, sketches and plays with great speed. At first, like so many writers, he had no success. But gradually he began to get his sketches published and his name became known.

His parents were extremely generous with money, and without their help he would probably have had to give up writing, for it was not until he was over thirty that he was offered an excellent job on the *Neue Freie Presse*, the most important Viennese newspaper. He was to go to Paris and act as special correspondent, sending news from France to Vienna. Herzl had grown very fond of Vienna; but he was a married man by now with a small son and two daughters, and the offer was too good to refuse, even though it meant making his home in another country.

Although as a boy and a young man he had taken no interest in Jewish affairs, the injustice with which Jews everywhere were now being treated was something that he could not avoid knowing and feeling. He had abandoned law because as a Jew his way to promotion was blocked; and earlier, while at the University of Vienna, he had resigned from a students' union because its members were antisemitic. He had read one of the books which had been written with the object of creating antisemitism. And more than once, while on a visit to Germany, he had been sneered at in the streets as a Jew. He had heard, too, the cry of "Hep, hep!":

it was a cry first used by the Crusaders as a signal for murdering the Jewish "infidels," and it was used now as a cry of derision.

Nobody could have looked less like the dejected, frightened Jew of the ghetto than Theodor Herzl. He was tall and elegantly dressed. With his great dark eyes, his clear-cut features and his thick black hair and beard, he reminded many people of some romantic monarch from the East: and there was something romantic in his nature, which matched the imposing dignity of his appearance.

Slowly his interest in his own people had been aroused; and in Paris for the first time he began to think of himself as a Jew, and of the Jews as one people. Fired by this sense of kinship, he wrote a play, *The New Ghetto*, the story of a brave and honest Jew who dies to defend his brother-Jews.

While Herzl was writing his play, an event occurred in France which showed to what appalling depths antisemitism could descend. In the autumn of 1894 he was ordered to report the trial of Captain Alfred Dreyfus for his newspaper. Dreyfus, a young Alsatian Jew, was on the French General Staff; and he had been arrested on a charge of selling French military secrets to Germany. The charge was utterly false, and the evidence against Dreyfus was forged. And yet he was convicted of treason, hounded out of the Army, and condemned to life imprisonment in the penal settlement on Devil's Island, off the coast of South America. Several years later Dreyfus' innocence was proved beyond all doubt. He was released, promoted to the rank of major, and awarded the French Legion of Honour. But the trial had produced a shocking outburst of antisemitism in France; and for a time the whole country seemed divided into two camps: in the one were the people who believed Dreyfus to be innocent; and in the other those who, despite all the evidence, continued to believe him guilty simply because he was a Jew.

If Herzl had not fully grasped it before, it was clear to him now that antisemitism was a deadly and dangerous force. In Western and Central Europe, it was true, the Jews were not actively persecuted or murdered, although they were living under considerable difficulties. But in Eastern Europe, particularly in Russia and Rumania, they lived in constant fear. In Russia, Jews were obliged to live within certain areas known as the Pale of Settlement; and there were laws which prevented them from educating their children except in Jewish schools and stopped them from taking any work under the government. They were, however, forced to do long terms of military service: they were heavily taxed: and on the slightest provocation they were murdered, their belongings stolen, their homes looted. In Rumania, too, the Jews were actively persecuted; and the only hope for thousands of Russian and Rumanian Jews lay in flight. Many Russian Jews—as we have seen—fled for safety to Britain or America: but at that time Russia alone had a population of nearly six million Jews, and no country was prepared to admit a very large number.

To Theodor Herzl, pondering seriously the plight of his unfortunate people, there seemed one obvious solution. The Jews must be given land of their own, a state in which they and their descendants could live in peace and security. In a fever of excitement he set down his ideas in writing, in a pamphlet which he called *Der Judenstaat—The Jewish State*. The Jews, he wrote, should be "granted sovereignty over a part of the globe large enough to satisfy the rightful claims of a nation." And he went on to describe the organization needed for such a state—a society of Jews to negotiate with the governments of the nations, and a Jewish company to deal with the general management and financial affairs of the state. He suggested two countries, either of which would be suitable for his Jewish state: the first was Palestine, the second Argentina in South America. Jewish public opinion and the Jewish Society, he said, would decide which of the two countries should be chosen.

In his ignorance of Jewish affairs, Herzl had no idea that his dream of a Jewish state was not new. It had been thought of many times through the ages; and in more modern times had been suggested nearly thirty years before—in 1862—

and again in 1882, by well-known Jewish thinkers. Had he realized this, he admitted later, he would never have written his pamphlet. Yet, this very ignorance was to lead, more than fifty years later, to the birth of the Jewish State of Israel. And Theodor Herzl, who was a man of action as well as a writer and a dreamer, provided the plan and prepared the way.

Carried away by excitement, Herzl had taken only a few weeks to write *The Jewish State*. He did not publish it straight away: he was uncertain how it would be received; and could not be sure if he had put his ideas in the right way. "I have the solution to the Jewish question," he said. "I know it sounds mad; and at the beginning I shall be called mad more than once—until the truth of what I am saying is recognized in all its shattering force." He was indeed thought mad. A friend, who was both doctor and journalist, went to see him soon after he had completed the pamphlet and was shocked at his appearance. Herzl, generally so well dressed and dignified, was untidy and unkempt, and looked as though he had not slept for weeks. He asked his friend to read the pamphlet in manuscript; and the friend, having read it, told him that the plan could only have been produced by a man with an overstrained mind. Herzl should consult a doctor without delay. "You are making a ridiculous—or a tragic— figure of yourself," his friend concluded, warning him that if he insisted on publishing his pamphlet he would cause his parents unhappiness and anxiety.

Dr. Herzl, who had already asked the learned Chief Rabbi of Vienna, Dr. Moritz Güdemann, to meet him and discuss his plan, wavered at the thought of causing unhappiness to his parents; and he asked his friend to send telegrams to Dr. Güdemann, and others to whom he had written, to cancel the invitation. He had begun to think that he really might be going mad when his friend came back with a bill for the telegrams. When he added up the total he found that the friend had made a mistake in his calculations; and this decided him that he was not mad but perfectly sane.

He therefore decided to go ahead with his plan. At first no one would take it seriously. But in Paris he met a well known Jewish writer and doctor, Max Nordau, who had drifted away from Judaism but who, like Herzl, had been brought back to it by the force of antisemitism. Nordau had no doubts at all about Herzl's sanity. He offered to help him, and became one of his strongest supporters in the struggle to come.

But Herzl still hesitated to publish his pamphlet: he wanted to make sure that his plan would be backed by at least one wealthy and influential Jew. So he approached Baron Maurice de Hirsch, one of the richest men of the day, who had made a fortune from railway construction. Baron de Hirsch had recently founded the Jewish Colonization Society (usually called the I.C.A.) with the object of settling oppressed Russian Jews in farming settlements in the Argentine and elsewhere in South America. He did not approve of the idea of founding a Jewish state: he was concerned only with providing the funds to support the settlements.

Turning aside from his quest for a wealthy supporter, Dr. Herzl, who realized how much he would need the help of leading rabbis, asked Dr. Güdemann if he might come and read his manuscript to him. A meeting was arranged in Munich, and the Chief Rabbi of Vienna brought with him a layman who was an expert on Jewish affairs. The three men lunched together at a Jewish restaurant and afterwards retired to a private room which the owner had put at their disposal. Herzl began to read. The others listened, interrupting sometimes with a critical remark; and after a short break during the afternoon, they met again in Herzl's hotel bedroom. It was a very small room and contained only two chairs, so Herzl sat on the bed and read aloud for another two hours. By dinnertime he had reached the very heart of his plan; and as they went down to the restaurant the Chief Rabbi said to him: "You seem to me like Moses." Herzl turned aside this praise with a laugh, but he was very much moved. And later in the evening, when they parted at the railway station, Dr. Güdemann kissed the younger man, saying: "Remain as you are. Perhaps you are the one chosen by God."

After this Herzl felt sure that he had gained an ally. He was wrong: Dr. Güdemann changed his mind; and when in due course *The Jewish State* was published he joined forces with those who attacked it.

Meanwhile, in the autumn of 1895, Herzl was recalled by his newspaper from Paris to Vienna and appointed Literary Editor. He held this appointment for the rest of his life: but his thoughts, his money, and every moment of his free time were given to the cause of his Jewish state. He overworked continually; for in order to provide for his family he went on writing plays. They were not very good plays, but when they were produced they brought him a certain amount of money; but he was well aware that he was never able to provide for *his* children as other fathers did for theirs.

All the same, he would let nothing deflect him from his plan. He turned next to England. Max Nordau gave him an introduction to the famous Jewish novelist Israel Zangwill, and the two men met in London. Conversation was difficult, for at that time Herzl understood very little English; yet Zangwill, who could speak no German, was captivated by Herzl's personality. At first he thought the plan was too far-fetched and romantic; but he suggested that Herzl should describe it to the Maccabæans, a club of Jewish professional men. A date was fixed: but, while the Maccabæans listened to Herzl politely, they were not impressed by what he said. He therefore decided to appeal to the Jewish public in an article which appeared in the London newspaper, *The Jewish Chronicle*. One month later—on February 14th, 1896 —*The Jewish State* was published as a pamphlet, first in German, then in English and French.

The fiercest argument broke out immediately. Some people came out on Herzl's side; but his supporters were far outnumbered by his opponents. His plan was opposed by those who believed that sooner or later all Jews would be able to merge themselves peacefully into the life of their countries; and also by those who clung to the idea that the Jews must remain in exile until the Messiah came to lead them back to the Holy Land. Rabbis and scholars were among those who accused Herzl of trying to create a new Jewish problem: and there were plenty of people to tell him that Jews would never be able to run an agricultural settlement successfully, because they were quite unsuited to working on the land.

To a group who called themselves Zionists and who were busy with plans to settle oppressed Jews from Russia in Palestine, Herzl's ignorance of what had already been achieved was amazing. Among them was a young Russian student, of whom we shall hear more later. His name was Chaim Weizmann and he was at that time studying in Berlin. "We had never heard of Herzl before," Chaim Weizmann wrote afterwards. "*The Jewish State* contained not a single new idea for us." He was shocked to discover that Herzl did not appear to know of the existence of the Lovers of Zion movement, nor of the word "Zionism" which had been given to the ideal for which they stood. Weizmann was shocked, too, because Herzl did not write of Palestine as the only goal and because he said nothing about the value of the Hebrew language.

All the same, if Weizmann and his friends of the Lovers of Zion found nothing new in Herzl's pamphlet, they were deeply impressed by his enthusiasm and daring. Only a man who was strong and sincere could have written it, a man who would not withdraw whatever the opposition. They decided to give him their support; and so did Zionist student groups in Austria and the Ukraine.

It was to the persecuted Jews of Eastern Europe that Herzl's plan made the most powerful appeal. His pamphlet was not allowed into Russia; yet somehow his name became known. This man, this new leader, who was said to resemble a prince of ancient Israel, would surely come, like Moses of old, to free them from bondage and lead them to the Promised Land. From Russia and Poland, from Bulgaria and Rumania, even from the Eastern European Jews who had settled in Palestine, calls came to Herzl for guidance and leadership.

In the East End of London, filled with Jewish emigrants

from Russia, a mass meeting was arranged in the summer of
1896. In the chair was Dr. Moses Gaster, Chief Rabbi of the
Sephardi community, who, unlike many important rabbis,
had announced his support of Herzl's cause. The hall was
filled to overflowing; thousands of Jews lined the East End
streets; and Herzl was cheered all along the route. When he
rose to speak it was borne in on him that to these fugitives
from Russia he was something more than a man: he was the
hero of a legend, although he had not meant to pose as one.

People might compare him with Moses; they might even
speak of him as the Messiah: but Herzl, while he could smile
at such romantic nonsense, was too deeply committed to
Zionism to turn back, and he was willing to take on the
leadership. By now he had given up all thoughts of a Jewish
state in the Argentine: it could be nowhere but in Palestine.
In order to give freedom to Zionist ideas he founded with
his own money a weekly journal *Die Welt—The World*. He
did so because the owners of the *Neue Freie Presse* refused
to print anything about Zionism and because many Jewish
papers criticized and attacked it. *Die Welt* came out with a
yellow cover. Yellow was chosen because in the Middle Ages
Jews had been forced to wear a distinguishing yellow badge;
and between the two words of the title appeared a Shield of
David and an outline map of the coast of Palestine.

At this time Herzl was also organizing a meeting, a congress of Zionists from all over the world. This was a bold
move; for opposition to the movement had been gathering
strength. Yet, on August 27th, 1897, 204 delegates gathered
in Basle in Switzerland to attend a three-day congress. They
belonged to every shade of Jewish thought; they ranged from
rabbis to businessmen, from scholars and students to workmen. And because they came from so many different
countries the speeches—which were given in German—had
to be translated into English, French, Russian and Yiddish.
Zionists, said Herzl in his opening speech, were coming
together as one people; and it was as one people that they
would return to their own land. He knew now what had
been happening in Palestine; and he spoke of the agricultural

settlements and of how Jews were proving that they could till and cultivate the land. But no settlement could prosper, he said, if its members relied on outside charity. Jews must learn to be self-supporting; to rely on their own efforts. And they must return to Palestine, not secretly and in small numbers, but openly and with the consent of the great Powers. The formation of a Jewish state in Palestine would strengthen the Turkish Empire, whose Sultan was still the overlord of Palestine; and the departure for Palestine of Jews from other countries would rid these countries of anti-semitism.

There were several other speakers at the Congress, among them Herzl's first helper, Max Nordau. But it was to Theodor Herzl that every one looked: to the distinguished-looking man with the dark eyes and the flowing black beard; with a clear and resonant voice, and a manner which seemed to fit him to speak for Zionism with kings and princes and the greatest men of the day.

At this first Zionist Congress a plan was drawn up and a Zionist Organization established. There was a single end in view: "The aim of Zionism is to create for the Jewish people a home in Palestine secured by public law." There should be a Zionist Society in every country; and these local societies should be joined in a Zionist Federation. Organization of the Federation was to be in the hands of a General Council (known as the Greater Actions Committee) made up of representatives from each country; and of a Central Executive (a smaller Actions Committee) whose members, like Herzl, lived in Vienna.

The Congress elected Theodor Herzl President of the Zionist Organization; and he wrote afterwards in his diary: "If I were to sum up the Basle Congress in one word—which I shall not do openly—it would be this: at Basle I founded the Jewish State. If I said so today, I should be greeted with general laughter. In five years, perhaps, and certainly in fifty, everybody will see it. The State is already founded, in essence, in the will of the people to the State." Herzl was too hopeful when he spoke of five years: it was to be fifty years almost to the day before the Jewish State of Israel came into being.

The proposed plan of the Basle Congress brought many new members to the Zionist movement, and societies were formed in every part of the world. There were still many influential Jews who opposed it. There were those, as we have seen, who believed that the Jews must patiently await the coming of the Messiah; and those who thought they could in time become secure and happy citizens of the countries in which they lived. There were also Jews who thought of themselves as a religious people, but not as members of a Jewish nation, in the ordinary sense of the word: and these people recalled that Palestine was holy not to the Jews alone but also to the Christians and, to a lesser extent, to the Moslems. They knew that it was the home of countless Moslem Arabs, who were afraid that if the Jews were allowed into the country they would be driven out. Both sides were sincere: but from now onwards the Zionist cause, with its appeal to the persecuted masses, gained steadily in strength.

During the next seven years five more Congresses were held, all of them in Basle except the fourth which was held in London. The number of delegates attending the second Congress was nearly double the number attending the first; and as Congress succeeded Congress it became clear that the Zionist movement was preparing for the creation of a really large settlement of Jews in Palestine. It was properly organized and large sums of money were being collected.

The London Congress brought many new recruits to the cause; and filled Herzl with hope that the British Government would support it. In London, Herzl had an interview with the Foreign Secretary, Lord Lansdowne, and found him interested in the movement. But the British Government was not pledged to help officially; and Herzl was now working on a scheme to gain the sympathy of the Sultan of Turkey. In 1901 he was granted an audience with the Sultan. The Turkish Empire, once so wealthy and powerful, had, as Herzl knew, lost much of its former wealth; and he suggested to the Sultan that he should be paid an annual tribute from Zionist funds if he would allow the Jews to settle freely in Palestine. For months the Sultan would not make up his mind: then he declared that he was willing for Jews to settle in parts of his Middle Eastern Empire, but not in Palestine. Herzl rejected the offer. "A Charter without Palestine!" he wrote in his diary. "I refused at once."

It was at the fifth Congress, held in 1901, that the very important question of the educational life of the Jews in a Jewish state was first debated. Chaim Weizmann, by this time one of the leaders of the movement, proposed that a Jewish University should be founded. "The dream of a Hebrew University in Jerusalem," Dr. Weizmann wrote later, "was born almost simultaneously with the Zionist movement"; and now, he thought, was the moment to bring it to life. Many of the other delegates considered that until the State was actually established it was quite pointless to talk about a university. But Herzl, although he felt that the State must come first, promised to try and obtain from the Sultan of Turkey a *firman* (order) which would permit a university to be founded. He failed; and told Weizmann that his idea would have to be shelved. Weizmann would not give way. "Our group," he wrote, "would not take no for an answer."

Although Weizmann admired his leader and realized that he was doing a great work, he disliked the atmosphere of hero-worship which surrounded him and Herzl's stately, rather grand manner. Weizmann himself was more down to earth and far more direct than Herzl. He often opposed him; but he respected him, especially for the understanding which he showed towards the Zionists from Russia, who were entirely different in character and ideas from the Zionists of Western Europe. The Russians might seem rough and uncultured; but Herzl was wise enough to perceive beneath their surface manner the learning and the ability which had brought them success "in a land where success is peculiarly difficult for the Jews."

While Dr. Weizmann and his friends "liked and admired

Dr. Herzl, and knew that he was a force in Israel," they did not approve of the way in which he journeyed about "interviewing the great of the world on our behalf." These interviews might sound important, thought Dr. Weizmann, but, in fact, they gained nothing. Before he visited the Sultan of Turkey in 1901, Herzl had had an audience with the Emperor of Germany, Kaiser William II, because he hoped the Emperor would support his appeal to the Sultan. This seemed to him likely when he first saw the Kaiser in Germany; and so, when he learned that the Emperor was going on a visit to Palestine, he decided to ask for a second audience in Jerusalem.

When Herzl arrived in Palestine he was received like a king by the colonists of the settlement of Rishon le-Zion, who were working desperately hard under the most difficult and unhealthy conditions. What he saw of the life of Rishon le-Zion made Herzl more convinced than ever that the Jewish problem could not be solved by the creation of settlements which depended for their existence on the charity of wealthy men. The problem would be solved only with the creation of an independent, self-supporting Jewish state. He met the Kaiser again; but although it seemed at first that the Kaiser would use his influence with the Sultan, in the end he did nothing about it.

A few years later, in 1904, Herzl went to Italy for an audience with King Victor Emmanuel III. The King seemed very sympathetic; and he asked to see a copy of *Altneuland*—or *The Old New Land*—the novel which Herzl had written on his dream of a colony in Palestine, and dedicated to the memory of his sister Pauline. Once again he pinned his hopes on a ruler; yet this interview, like the others, achieved nothing. While he was in Italy Herzl was also received by the Pope; and from the Pope he received a decisive "no." "If you go to Palestine," said the Pope, " and settle your people there, we shall need to have churches and priests ready to baptise every one of you."

A visit to Russia proved rather more useful, for Herzl managed to gain from the Minister of the Interior an

assurance that, for the time being at any rate, the work of
the Zionists—which had come under Government suspicion
—should not be interfered with. On his homeward journey
he stopped at Vilna; and there, to the alarm of the police,
the entire Jewish population turned out to greet him. The
police forbade all demonstrations; but they could not prevent
Herzl's reception by the leaders of the Jewish community,
who blessed him and presented him with addresses of praise
and welcome. A banquet was secretly prepared for him at a
village a few miles beyond the town; and on the way Herzl
asked to see the houses where the poorest Jews lived. When
he was shown their wretched hovels he was so moved that
he wept. And he was no less moved by the dignity of a poor
Jew to whom he offered a gold coin. The man refused to
take the money. All he desired, he said, was to see Dr.
Herzl.

After the banquet Herzl went straight to the railway
station, driving through streets lined with his people. At the
station a crowd of admirers awaited him: but the police
dispersed them with careless brutality. Pale and horrified at
what he had seen, Herzl begged those of his friends who
had been allowed to bid him goodbye never to lose hope.
"Better times are coming," he assured them. "Better times
must come. That is what we are working for."

It had become clear in the meantime that there was more
sympathy in Britain for the Zionist cause than elsewhere.
It seemed possible that the British Government would press
for the founding of a Jewish colony in the Sinai Peninsula
or the island of Cyprus—which might be used as a spring-
board to Palestine. Both these plans failed: the Cyprus plan
because the inhabitants objected, the Sinai Peninsula plan
because the land was very dry and the Egyptian authorities
refused to allow the waters of the River Nile to be used to
irrigate it.

Then the British Colonial Secretary, Joseph Chamberlain,
came forward with a more definite suggestion. He had
recently returned from East Africa: and, "on my travels,"
he told Herzl, "I saw the very country for you. It is hot on

the coast of East Africa, but inland the climate is excellent for Europeans. You can grow cotton and sugar there. I thought to myself: 'That's just the country for Dr. Herzl. But *he* must have Palestine and will not move unless he can settle in or near it.' "

"Yes, I must," Herzl replied. "Our base must be in or near Palestine." Later on, he added, there might be a settlement in East Africa as well.

This was his own opinion: he could not accept or reject the offer officially until he had consulted the delegates to the next Zionist Congress. Although he would have liked to turn down any offer of land in East Africa, some of his friends—Max Nordau among them—were so concerned with the threat of massacre which hung permanently over the Jews of Eastern Europe that they begged him to think of the consequences. An East African offer should be accepted, they urged, at any rate as a temporary solution.

A few months earlier there had been a particularly cold-blooded massacre of Jews in Kishinev in Russia; and, fearing that this massacre would be followed by others as bad or worse, Herzl agreed to his friends' suggestion. In August, 1903, he went to the Zionist Congress at Basle to urge acceptance, or at least consideration, of Britain's idea. He was greeted with an outburst of criticism and abuse. He had reckoned on opposition; but he had never imagined that the strongest criticism would come from the Russian delegates, representatives of the people who stood to suffer most if the offer were to be rejected. When Herzl and Nordau pressed that the offer should be accepted, at any rate temporarily, the Russian delegates indignantly refused. The speakers were standing in front of a map of East Africa which had been hung on the wall instead of the usual map of Palestine. And feeling was so strong that when the first session of the Congress was suspended, a young woman rushed up the steps to the platform and defiantly tore down the map.

When the debate was resumed it was agreed—by 295 votes to 178—that the offer should be examined. At this, the

Russian delegates left the hall, some of them weeping with indignation and despair.

Chaim Weizmann was one of those who considered that the mere idea of considering any territory except Palestine was treachery to the cause. In the months which followed opposition to the East African scheme grew until there was grave danger of a split in the Zionist movement; and more than once Herzl was called by the ugly word "traitor."

When he realized how strong the opposition was Herzl gave way. At a meeting of the Greater Actions Committee held in Vienna on April 11th, 1904, he vowed that he would always be faithful to the ideal of a Jewish state in Palestine. He had, he said, learned much about Jews and about Jewish ideals during his years as leader of the Zionist movement. "But above all, I learned to understand that we shall find the solution of our problem only in Palestine. . . . If today I say to you, 'I became a Zionist, and have remained one, and all my efforts are directed toward Palestine,' you have every reason in the world to believe me."

This meeting was the last Herzl ever attended. He had been torn by the discord within the movement and the mistrust which had been shown him. He was only forty-four; but he was a tired man now and a very sick one; and for a long time his friends had feared for his health. He had never spared himself, but by the summer of 1904 he was feeling so ill that he agreed to go to North Austria for a rest cure. He was too late; for on July 3rd, quietly and without pain, he died.

Theodor Herzl had served the cause of Zionism only for eight years; yet in that brief time he had shaped the movement which years later was to bring his people home. He had planned with foresight; for when the time came there was no hesitation on the part of the nations concerned in trusting in the ability of the Zionist Organization to establish the Jewish State. Today, more than fifty years after his death, Israeli citizens look on Herzl as the real founder of Israel.

LEO BAECK
(1873-1956)
A Hero of Our Times

VERY early one morning about eighty years ago, a five-year-old boy and his father set out on a long walk. They were going to see the first railway line to be opened in their district, and they were so anxious not to miss the first train that they ran the last part of the way, arriving at the barrier out of breath. They waited for a few minutes and then the train roared past without stopping. To the man the railway was an invention which would bring people closer together and bring about a better understanding between them. The boy, who felt the excitement of the moment keenly, was to travel frequently by train and even by air in his old age. But to him, the best way to bring people near to one another was always to walk and talk with them. When he grew up, one of his greatest gifts was his understanding of people with widely differing points of view and his ability to draw the best from them.

The boy's name was Leo Baeck. He was the seventh of a family of eleven children; and his father, Samuel Baeck, was Rabbi of the Jewish congregation of the little town of Lissa in the East German province of Posen (which today is Poznan, a province of Poland). Rabbi Baeck was a scholar and a historian, and his wife was the granddaughter of a well-known German rabbi. Poles as well as Germans lived in Lissa—Roman Catholics, Protestants and Jews; and although there were often differences between them, they lived peacefully enough together.

The Baeck children had a very happy childhood; and they never met the sneers and unkindness which Jews were suffering in other parts of Germany and Europe. They lived in a house which was rented to their father by one of the Protestant ministers—a follower of the creed laid down by the sixteenth-century reformer, John Calvin. Although the value of the house increased as the years went by and the rents of other houses in Lissa went up, the rent of Rabbi Baeck's house was never raised. The Calvinist minister's kindness to the minister of another faith was something that Leo Baeck never forgot: and the mingling of nations and religions in Lissa helped to make him tolerant and understanding.

Leo Baeck's first teacher was his father, who started when his son was three or four years old to teach him the traditions of his own faith. When the boy was older he went to the local grammar school, where Jews and Christians all felt part of the school community. It had always been understood that Leo would become a rabbi; and he completed his education first at a Jewish theological college in Breslau and then in Berlin, where he studied theology, history and philosophy. In Berlin he encountered the spirit of a recent movement in Judaism—the Reform Movement. The founders of this movement, which had started in Germany in the early part of the nineteenth century, believed that while the importance of Judaism remains the same for all time, some of the ritual and practices which had grown up around it held no meaning in modern surroundings. From reform grew other movements which teach that Judaism is eternal but that its message may grow and develop from age to age. These movements, together with the Reform Movement from which they sprang, are known today as Progressive Judaism and have formed congregations in all parts of the world.

Leo Baeck became a rabbi in the Reform Movement; and he found in Progressive Judaism the inspiration of his whole life. To him, as to the other reformers, it was the spirit of

Judaism which counted. "Great Judaism is more than a few little Judaisms," he said: and he claimed that Jews must give the Jewish answer, in line with Jewish history and tradition, to the problems which confront mankind.

The first congregation Leo Baeck served was at Oppeln in Silesia. He stayed in Oppeln for ten years and then spent five years with a larger congregation at Düsseldorf. He married a wife whom he loved dearly; and they had one daughter. The children in the religious school at Oppeln found their Rabbi a magnificent teacher. They loved and revered him, although he sometimes became impatient with a pupil who was lazy or wilfully stupid. In after years, when Dr. Baeck had become famous, one of them recalled with pride that he had once been slapped by the great man! This had had some effect; for, although he was rather lazy over his work in other subjects, the boy gained such high marks for religious subjects in his final school examinations that he got through on the strength of his religious knowledge.

The things Dr. Baeck told the children, even the simplest things, remained in their memory long after they had grown up and gone out into the world. Speaking once about the symbols for the various festivals, he told them that the festival of *Shavuot* (or Pentecost) always reminded him of the new suit which he wore every year for the first time during the festival. One year when he was quite small wearing his brand-new suit he went for a walk with an old family maid. They came to a ditch which Leo decided to jump; but his foot slipped and he fell into the muddy water at the bottom. He clambered out, covered with mud, and very upset because his parents would think him careless. But the understanding maid hurried him home and cleaned the suit so well that no one noticed that anything had happened to it.

Except when speaking to the children—who were more likely to remember important events when personal stories were attached to them—Dr. Baeck never used the personal pronoun "I" from the pulpit. He had no intention of using his own personality and his experiences as an object-lesson to his congregation: he would not use them, as many preachers do in their sermons, to illustrate a point or explain the growth of a truth. He did not want his congregation simply to sit back and listen: he wanted them to exert their minds and apply their own intelligence to what he said. He spoke and wrote of a truth with the authority that comes from knowledge; but when he felt that he lacked the authority or the truth, he remained silent. His preaching made rather heavy demands on his congregation but it brought out the best in them. Only once did he break his rule—on the occasion of his farewell sermon at Oppeln. The subject of his sermon was Moses' farewell to the Children of Israel before he climbed Mount Nebo to see before he died the wonders of the Promised Land. "Never," said Dr. Baeck, "has the word 'I' been spoken in this pulpit; but today as I say goodbye I will use it." In his quiet, rather hesitant voice, which was yet clear and penetrating, he gave one of his finest sermons; and partly because they were so unused to hearing their Rabbi speak of himself his congregation never forgot it.

The whole congregation missed him when he left Oppeln for Düsseldorf, especially the children, who made life difficult at first for his successor. "The *Herr Doktor* said this," they told their new Rabbi, or, "the *Herr Doktor* did it that way"; for to them there was only one *Herr Doktor* in the world. Dr. Baeck, tall, slight, somewhat frail-looking and inclined to stoop, with large, expressive eyes behind his spectacles, was remembered by the children for his friendliness and understanding; for he never talked down to his pupils, but treated them all as his equals. Their parents also thought of him as a friend, and remembered his modesty, his courtesy, and the true humility which is shown by the very great. They did not think of him as an heroic figure: he seemed too gentle and self-effacing. But he possessed those qualities which made heroes of the Jewish leaders of old: utter faith in God and his religion, which gave him a sense of security and confidence and made him completely fearless. In the days to come he was to prove himself as great a hero as any one of them.

Dr. Baeck was nearly forty when he was called to Berlin and left Düsseldorf to serve as rabbi of a very large congregation and to lecture at the *Hochschule*—the Academy for the study of Judaism where he had finished his own education. This was an important position for a man who was still quite young; but during the past few years Dr. Baeck had become famous as a scholar and writer. He had written a book, which was later translated into many languages and revised many times, and which was being read by Jewish and Christian scholars all over the world. It was called *The Essence of Judaism;* and he wrote it in reply to a book by a Christian scholar in which Judaism as a great religion had not even been mentioned. Like Moses Mendelssohn before him in a somewhat similar situation, Baeck replied not with anger but with gentleness and tact. But he went much further than Mendelssohn. His book did not simply defend his own beliefs: it was a clear, positive, and profound expression of the thought and teachings of the Judaism which inspired him. It is a book to which scholars return again and again; for it is so filled with wisdom that every sentence gives rise to thought. As a Reform rabbi of today puts it: "A sermon could be based on every one of them." Leo Baeck wrote a number of other books in the course of his life; but the *Essence*, which he worked on so many times through the years, remains the most important.

Except for an interval during the War of 1914-18 when he served as a chaplain to the German forces, Dr. Baeck remained in Berlin for many years. He was a brilliant lecturer; and, as one of his students wrote: "His subject never becomes mere knowledge, he transforms it into real life." Although he was so busy with his duties as a rabbi and a lecturer, as well as with his studies and writing, Dr. Baeck was soon taking a leading part in the affairs of his people all over Germany, and before long with the affairs of Jews all over the world. He was not a Zionist, but he looked with hope towards the National Home in Palestine. To him, what mattered most was that a Jew should be a good Jew and a good man; and he could be as good a Jew in Germany or anywhere else as he could in Palestine. Among the causes he worked for was the Order of B'nai B'rith, the Jewish organization with headquarters in the United States which seeks to unite in brotherhood Jews of all kinds of opinion and to give help to those in need. Dr. Baeck was Grand President of the Order for Germany, and also President of the Union of German Rabbis : and people inside Germany and beyond began to look on him as the leading representative of German Jewry.

His home soon became a meeting-place for rabbis and scholars from all parts of the world; and he and his wife kept open house for their many friends. His daughter today looks back on her girlhood as a wonderfully happy time. Her parents had up-to-date ideas about education and she was brought up in a modern way. Her father, to whom she was especially devoted, taught her religious knowledge and Hebrew; and with his encouragement she studied to become a doctor. Then she married; and later on Dr. Baeck was teaching a granddaughter the history of her religion.

But by this time a dark threat to their happiness and indeed to their lives was drawing very near. After the war of 1914-18 hatred of the Jews was revived. Times were bad. Germany had been defeated; and defeated nations are generally inclined to put the blame for defeat on others. Among the people who could not—or would not—face the responsibility for what had happened was a young Austrian workman called Adolf Hitler. Excitable and often tearful, Hitler was as cruel as the tyrants of ancient times. He easily convinced his political party that all Germany's troubles were due to the Jews. The wicked Jews, he claimed, had stabbed the victorious armies in the back, turning certain German victory into defeat. The fact that the Jews were completely innocent and nobody could explain how they had stabbed Germany in the back did not matter at all to Hitler and his friends. They had found their victim: the Jews were to pay for Germany's defeat. They were also to pay for the success they had achieved as doctors, lawyers, and teachers, as financiers and men of commerce, and in all the other professions.

At first Hitler had little influence; but a shortage of goods and employment was causing people to lose faith in their Government and to turn instead towards Communism or towards Hitler's party, the National Socialist Party—the Nazi Party, as it was called. This was Hitler's chance. By the force of his voice and his personality, evil though it was, he had drawn more and more Germans to his side; and his influence was so strong that they were willing to follow him blindly. In 1933 Hitler climbed to power as Chancellor of Germany. A year later he had become the Führer—the acknowledged Leader of the country.

The Jews had watched Hitler's rise with growing fear; but they could do nothing to prevent it. Dr. Baeck, deeply concerned at this terrible threat to his people, was greatly troubled also at the lack of true religion among the Germans, a lack which had made Hitler's rise possible. Some years before Hitler came to power Dr. Baeck had written to a friend: "We discover two roots of our being within ourselves. Every man is a citizen of two worlds. From this fact there must follow tasks and conflicts for every human being. All martyrdom results from it. Men belong to the realm of the state and to the realm of God. Which law shall they obey when a conflict occurs?"

To Leo Baeck the choice was simple. Come what may, he would choose the law of God. But many of the leaders of Germany, as he knew only too well, were unconscious of the choice; for they had turned the very fact of being German into a religion.

Very soon after Hitler became Führer it was clear that the Jews were to be shown no mercy. They were not, he declared, of "pure" German blood; and they were to be made to answer for the troubles and the faults of the whole nation. In many German cities Jews were seized and beaten up by Hitler's thugs. Their jobs were taken away from them; their shops were looted; they were refused admission to the universities; forbidden to study law or medicine or to become journalists. Those who could afford to do so and those who realized that they could be of service to other countries began to leave Germany. But without great talents or money it was difficult to gain admission anywhere.

Germany had a large Jewish population; and the task of their spiritual leaders, said Dr. Baeck, was "to get ready for what might lie ahead." He therefore called the leaders together to Berlin to talk over a course of action. A two-fold plan was agreed: as many children and young people as possible should be sent away to safety; and for those who remained the comforts of religion and learning should be freely available.

To help those Jews who were able to emigrate to leave the country and to make conditions more bearable for those who had to stay, a Representative Council of German Jews was set up; and Leo Baeck was appointed President. He thus became the official leader of the Jews and their spokesman with the Nazis. The members of the Council did wonderful work. They were distinguished men and women who could easily have found refuge in other countries; but they preferred to stay in Germany and help. They worked under extreme difficulties. They were seldom allowed to hold their meetings in private, for Nazi officials were generally present taking notes of everything that was said. Dr. Baeck as their leader bore the heaviest responsibility. Some people, even among his friends, thought at first that he was too gentle, too prone to see both sides of a question, and too much inclined to compromise to be able to win any concessions from the Nazis. They soon found out that they were mistaken. Dr. Baeck never spoke with Nazi officials unless it was absolutely necessary. When he did speak he showed his anger at what they were doing by treating them with that exaggerated form of politeness which is very like contempt. Despite themselves, the Nazis began to respect him. He realized their power; but he was quite clearly not afraid. Several times they arrested him and took him away for questioning; but each time he was released.

Conditions for the Jews became worse in 1935, when the shamelessly unjust Nuremberg Laws were passed. These laws deprived the Jews of all their rights and privileges as

German citizens; and they were made to apply equally to Jews who had become Christians and to those who were faithful to their religion. Jews were not allowed to share the special winter relief which was given to other Germans; and as many of them had been deprived of their jobs they had no means of support. If an appeal for funds had not been permitted in the synagogues many would have starved that winter.

To hearten his frightened and despairing people Dr. Baeck had composed a prayer to be said in synagogues all over the country on the solemn Eve of the Day of Atonement. "In this hour," he wrote, "every man in Israel stands erect before his Lord, the God of justice and mercy, to open his heart in prayer. Before God we will question our ways and search our deeds, the acts we have done and those we have left undone. We will publicly confess the sins we have committed and beg the Lord to pardon and forgive. Acknowledging our trespasses, individual and communal, let us despise the slanders and calumnies directed against us and our faith. Let us declare them lies, too mean and senseless for our reckoning." He wrote too of the grandeur of Jewish history and of how, from generation to generation, God had redeemed and rescued His people from oppression. "Our prayer is the prayer of all Jews; our faith is the faith of all Jews living on the earth. When we look into the faces of one another, we know who we are; and when we raise our eyes heavenward, we know eternity is within us. For the Guardian of Israel neither slumbers nor sleeps."

Services in the synagogues were closely watched by the Nazis, who interfered in advance to prevent the prayer being read. Dr. Baeck must have realized what would happen; but despite the Nazis the contents of the prayer became known and were even quoted in the newspapers of other countries. He had also made plain to the Nazis what he thought of the lies and the slanders directed against his faith. He was taking a risk when he signed the prayer, and he knew it. Arrested again and questioned, he was released after twenty-four hours.

The passing of the Nuremberg Laws led to more active persecution of the Jews. Concentration camps were constructed where Jews and other "enemies" of the Nazis, many of whom had never before done manual work, were forced to toil so hard that numbers of them died. In the summer of 1938 Dr. Baeck signed a document which described in detail what was happening in one of these concentration camps and the loss of innocent Jewish lives. He sent the document to Nazi headquarters, heedless of the risk he ran.

In the autumn of the same year 12,000 Jews who lived on the borders of Germany and Poland were thrust across the German frontier. Their way was barred by a barbed wire fence, and the Poles would not admit them. They could not go forward and they could not go back; and in the open, in the cold of autumn, many died from exposure or starvation, while others went mad. The son of one of these pitiful couples, who had escaped from Germany and gone to France, made up his mind to stage a protest. He went to the German Embassy in Paris and shot and killed a German official. The Nazis immediately declared that the whole of German Jewry was responsible for the crime which had been committed by a single Jew, half-crazed by the sufferings of his people. It gave them the excuse they wanted to murder innocent Jews in their hundreds; to levy an impossibly heavy fine on the survivors; to burn down synagogues; to send Jews in droves to the concentration camps. Dr. Baeck knew only too well that any appeal for justice or mercy would be in vain; yet he signed a letter of protest to the Nazis. Never would he add to an injustice by seeming to condone it. When the Nazis closed down the B'nai B'rith and confiscated its property they arrested Dr. Baeck as Grand Master. They brought to his cell a statement for his signature in which he agreed to cede the property to the Government. He refused to sign it. "Thus," he said, "their act stood as the theft which it was." Once more Dr. Baeck was released to take up his heart-breaking work.

Despite the anxiety and the constant danger he could still find comfort in study and writing; and during these troubled years he translated the Christian Gospels from Greek into Hebrew. In 1937 he had suffered a deep personal sorrow: his dearly loved wife died, her death hastened by her constant fears for her husband's safety.

Since the massacre which followed the shooting of the German official in Paris it had become more and more necessary for Jews—if they were not to be killed—to leave Germany, and also Austria, which was under Nazi rule. Other countries took as many refugees as their Governments would allow; and groups of children were welcomed, especially in England.

Among the families who found a home in England were Dr. Baeck's daughter with her husband and child. When the child first went to an English school she could scarcely believe that she would not be taunted for being Jewish or forbidden to take part in school activities. "I am so happy," she said, "because I can do everything the other girls do."

Dr. Baeck, who had many English friends, had been sure that his family would be happy. When some friends who had been expelled by the Nazis came to say goodbye to him before they left, he reminded them that England was a Christian country and that there they would find help. "Everybody who goes to England," he told them, "finds a helper."

There were many famous people among the fugitives: the great physicist Albert Einstein, a friend of Leo Baeck's, was one of them. There were doctors and scientists, writers, lawyers, and skilled workers; and, just as in the days of old when Jews fled from murder and persecution, their skill and industry enriched the countries which offered them shelter.

Einstein went to the United States, which was ready to take a large number of fugitives. But with the approach of the 1939 war it became increasingly difficult to get from Europe to America; and when war was declared those unfortunate Jews who had not been able to escape from Germany were caught in a trap.

For Dr. Baeck escape would have been easy. He was well known in Europe and America, and several important appointments were offered him. He refused them all. The Jews in Germany needed him now more than ever; and he would not abandon them. Friends in England were especially anxious to make a home for him; and when, before the war, he came to London to discuss plans for the reception of German-Jewish children, they hoped they might persuade him to stay. Gently but with absolute firmness, he answered: "I must go back." He went; and his friends feared they had said goodbye to him for ever.

In Germany also he was urged to leave. An adventurous Scotsman, Sir Michael Bruce, who had started an organization to help the Jews to escape from Austria and Germany, tells in his book, *Tramp Royal*, how he met Dr. Baeck and Mr. Wilfrid Israel, owner of one of Berlin's largest department stores, who had been going around the city doing what he could for the frightened Jews. Sir Michael arranged for the two men to be flown to safety in a private plane and came to tell them. "I will go when the Rabbi goes," said Mr. Israel. "And I," added Dr. Baeck, "will go when I am the last Jew alive in Germany."

Just before war broke out Dr. Baeck accepted the presidency of the World Union for Progressive Judaism. If the Nazis had not realized before that he was respected by Jews all over the world they knew it now; and the knowledge enraged them. Yet still, although they arrested him no fewer than five times, they let him go after questioning; and quietly and calmly he went on with his tasks, aiding and comforting his stricken people; playing for time with the Nazis—priceless time which enabled more people to escape.

Although he feared that for the trapped Jewish community there was little hope of survival once war had begun, Dr. Baeck was even more certain that the evil of Nazism would one day destroy itself, as indeed it did. Not every German was tainted with the evil; and he was heartened not only by Jewish heroism and endurance but also by examples of Christian kindness. It was a risky thing to show kindness to a Jew; but after the death of Dr. Baeck's wife the maid who had been with them throughout their married life stayed on as his housekeeper. The Nazi secret police—the Gestapo—called several times and told her that as a good German she had no right to work for a Jew; but she declined to go.

The Jews were forced—as Jews in the Middle Ages had been forced—to wear a distinguishing yellow badge in the form of the Star of David. They were kept on very short rations; and some Germans showed their sympathy by bringing them food secretly. Every Friday a basket of vegetables, which could not be bought on the Jewish ration card, was delivered at Dr. Baeck's front door, and sometimes he also received a gift of fruit. One day in a crowded tram a man, noticing his yellow badge, pressed close to Dr. Baeck and asked him the name of the next stop, adding in a whisper: "I am up from the country and I have just put a few eggs in your pocket." Another day in the street a passer-by dropped an envelope. He picked it up and handed it to Dr. Baeck, saying: "You dropped this." The envelope contained a packet of ration stamps.

As President of the Representative Council of German Jews, Dr. Baeck was often summoned before the Gestapo to receive orders. When the Nazi official in charge saw Dr. Baeck wearing his yellow badge for the first time he felt some embarrassment, perhaps even a glimmer of shame, and hastened to justify the order. "Well, Dr. Baeck," he said, "even you cannot deny that the German nation approves the Führer's actions, including his policy towards the Jews." "I should not like to comment on that point," replied Dr. Baeck. "But I will say this: when I walk back I shall not come to any harm—I am quite sure of that. Every now and then somebody will come up to me, a stranger, a little scared of being watched, who will grasp my hand. Perhaps he will slip an apple into my pocket, a bar of chocolate or even a cigarette. Apart from this I don't think anything will happen to me." He paused, then added: "I do not know whether the Führer, were he in my place, would find the same thing happening to him." Few people would have dared to make such a remark; but there was a dignity and strength in Dr. Baeck's bearing which even the Nazis found impressive. "Although I never bent," he said afterwards, "sometimes even taking risks and being threatened with arrest, those in power, strangely enough, always treated me with a certain respect and often acquiesced in my refusing to yield to their demands."

In the first years of the war, as Germany overran first one European country and then another, the Nazis enforced in German-occupied territory all the savage laws against the Jews. In these countries too there were courageous Christians who were ready to hide Jews in their houses, feed them, and man underground escape routes. In Denmark King Christian X made a gallant gesture. When the Nazis ordered all Danish Jews to wear the yellow badge the King declared that if the order were enforced he himself and every member of his Government would wear the Star of David. And Danes, at great risk to their lives, gathered together as many Jews as they could and smuggled them secretly out of Denmark to the safety of neutral Sweden.

There were many acts of heroism among the Jews. Perhaps the finest display of courage was shown by 60,000 Polish Jews who were besieged by the Nazis in the old Warsaw ghetto. The year was 1943, and by this time the Nazis had invented swifter and more dreadful means of ridding themselves of the Jews than overwork and starvation in the concentration camps. They deported them to special camps in Poland where they were murdered in gas chambers or by injections. The Warsaw Jews, threatened with deportation, refused to leave the ghetto. They had armed themselves with every weapon they could find, and when the Nazis attacked the ghetto they returned their fire. For five long weeks, weak and hungry as they were, the Jews held out. When at last the Nazis broke into the ghetto not a single Jew remained alive; for each man had fought until he was killed.

After the war two large rubberized milkcans were dug up from the ruins of the ghetto. In them was found a collection of notes (which has since been published) describing the whole history of the Warsaw ghetto and its inhabitants during those terrible years. The notes had been compiled by a Polish-Jewish historian, Emmanuel Ringelblum, and a small band of voluntary helpers, and carefully buried. Ringelblum, who knew that he could not survive, was writing not for himself but for posterity. This gay and humorous young man was one of the heroes of the war. He need not have died, for he need never have entered the ghetto at all. At the outbreak of war he was in Switzerland attending the twenty-first Zionist Congress: but he had insisted on returning to Warsaw to do relief work among his fellow-Jews and to carry out his self-appointed task of letting the world know the full story of Nazi crime and Jewish heroism. "Though we are condemned to die," he had written, "we have not lost our human faces."

Leo Baeck was another hero who never lost his human face—his humanity—even in the hour of his fiercest trial. Very early one morning in January, 1943, the bell of his front door rang. His housekeeper answered the door and ushered in two Gestapo officials. They had orders, they told Dr. Baeck, to arrest him and take him to the concentration camp of Theresienstadt in Czechoslovakia. This time, as he knew, he would not merely be questioned and released. He replied that he would be ready in an hour. Curtly, they said he must accompany them at once. "If you insist," answered Dr. Baeck, "you will have to carry me through the streets." The Nazis gave him the hour. He spent it writing a farewell letter to friends in neutral Portugal who would—as they had done previously—send it on to its proper destination, to his daughter in London. He also settled his small outstanding bills. "As we say in Germany," he remarked afterwards, "one likes to leave with a clean shirt."

Dr. Baeck was nearly seventy when he was taken to Theresienstadt. With his stoop and his white beard he looked very frail, and his friends feared that he could not live long. When news of his arrest reached Palestine it was thought that even now he might be rescued. There was some talk in Jerusalem of an exchange plan to be organized by the Roman

Catholic Church for the sake of German churchmen who were gallantly defying the Nazis. Dr. Baeck's friends called on the Roman Catholic Cardinal in Jerusalem and asked him if anything could be done for the Rabbi. The Cardinal, obviously deeply moved by their story, answered with kindness and sympathy: "My friends, your mission is in vain. If the man is such as you have described him, he will never desert his flock."

Theresienstadt was not a death camp, but many people died there. Three of Dr. Baeck's sisters had already perished, and a fourth died soon after his arrival. The high death rate was caused by the appalling living conditions; for 45,000 Jews were herded into barracks which had been built for 3,000 soldiers. Bunks were built in tiers with so little space between that it was impossible to sit upright. Food was bad and very scarce; there was so little water for washing and such shocking sanitary arrangements that the prisoners were soon infested with vermin and suffering from the diseases caused by dirt. "Treatment in Theresienstadt," said Dr. Baeck with gentle sarcasm, "was better than in most camps, where the victims were killed quickly. The people of Theresienstadt were allowed to die slowly."

In Theresienstadt the people were always hungry, hungry not only for food but for the things of the mind and spirit. There were very few books in the camp, for most of the prisoners' belongings were stolen by the guards; and people would gladly exchange a slice of bread for the loan of a book.

The Nazis made Dr. Baeck a member of the so-called Council of Elders, which gave him a position of some authority. He used it to console and strengthen the prisoners. At first he was made to do humiliating work. Side by side with another prisoner he was tethered like a beast of burden to a heavy refuse cart; yet as they dragged the cart the two elderly men rose above the humiliation and discussed philosophy. After Dr. Baeck's seventieth birthday he was relieved of menial tasks; and this left him free to minister to all those who needed his help, the living, the sick and the dying. By his own sure faith he rekindled faith in others: and one old friend—a member of his first congregation at Oppeln—said that whenever she saw Dr. Baeck in the camp she could believe that one day everything would be well.

Dr. Baeck could never exist for long without writing; and in Theresienstadt he wrote a book called *The Jewish People*. He worked on it in secret and, as he had no writing-paper, he used toilet paper. He was one of a number of distinguished scholars from Germany and the German-occupied countries; and under his direction they banded together to give the other prisoners a series of lectures. Dr. Baeck, whose memory was so good that he needed no reference books, lectured on the Bible and its commentaries and on the Greek and Hebrew philosophers, Moses Maimonides among them. Seven or eight hundred people squeezed themselves into the attic of one of the barracks to listen to the lectures; and so eager were they to hear that they forgot the cold and their misery, forgot their fears for the future, and—as Dr. Baeck put it—"they clustered on the bunks like grapes on a vine." Many of them were doomed to die; but in these hours of contentment they found the freedom of the mind and spirit which overcomes fear.

The Nazi officials did not intervene to put a stop to the lectures; but they had made it a rule that no education at all should be given to the children in the camp. Somehow or other, cautiously and in secret, the children were taught, until the day came when every single child in Theresienstadt could read and write.

A religious service was held whenever people asked for it; and Dr. Baeck said prayers every morning and evening. He understood then more strongly than ever before "how utterly dependent man is upon faith." And he spoke too of "the strength and pleasure" which he and his congregation "got from our Judaism, from the reading of the Bible and from the study of our Jewish tradition."

Perhaps Dr. Baeck's greatest achievement in the mud and misery of Theresienstadt was to give to the men and women who were condemned to die the strength and courage to face death with dignity. At intervals groups of prisoners were rounded up and deported to one of the death camps. In two months alone some 25,000 were deported; and when one batch of prisoners left another arrived from Nazi-occupied Europe.

Each time a group of condemned Jews left Theresienstadt Dr. Baeck expected an order to accompany them; yet each time he was left behind. He could not understand why this should be; for he was well known at Nazi headquarters. It must have been harder for him to stay than to go. Strong in his faith, he had no fear of death; and it would have been easier to die than to have to say farewell to group after group of his doomed congregation.

He faced death often enough, for epidemics of deadly diseases broke out in the camp, and the sick and the dying needed his help. But although he was old and looked delicate, he had always been healthy. Towards the end of the war in Europe the Nazis sent trainloads of people suffering from typhus into Theresienstadt, hoping that they would infect the survivors with the deadly disease. In an effort to prevent the spread of infection, the Council of Elders tried to isolate the sick in separate barracks; but the sick, in their fever and misery, threatened to break out. Dr. Baeck went alone into the isolation barracks and faced an angry, rebellious mob. He told them that if they would remain in isolation and accept the medical treatment which the camp could provide he would gladly stay with them. His willingness to risk certain infection calmed the sick. They agreed to do as he asked: and although it was not possible to prevent the spread of infection altogether, some who would otherwise have died of typhus lived to see the day of liberation.

The mystery of Dr. Baeck's survival was solved one day when Adolf Eichmann, one of the worst of the Nazi persecutors, paid a surprise visit to Theresienstadt. When he saw Dr. Baeck, whom he had known as President of the Representative Council, he was visibly taken aback. "Herr Baeck," he exclaimed in surprise, "are you still alive? I thought you were dead."

"Herr Eichmann," replied Dr. Baeck, "you appear to be bringing me some good news."

"I understand," said Eichmann grimly. "The man who is presumed to be dead is given longer to live."

The reason why Dr. Baeck's death had been presumed was that the death of a rabbi named Beck had been reported, and the Nazis had confused the names. Now that they realized their mistake Dr. Baeck's death was only a matter of time. He was fully prepared for it; confident and serene as ever.

Yet death did not come. The war was almost over: the Nazis had been defeated; and during the next few days the sound of guns was heard in the camp. As the Allied armies—British, American, and Russian—advanced into Germany it fell to the Russians to liberate Theresienstadt, and as they approached the Nazi guards fled in panic before them.

When the Russians entered Theresienstadt on May 12th, 1945, only 600 Jews were still alive. In the other concentration camps the same dreadful story was repeated: and when the terrible total of deaths was published the world knew that some five million Jews had perished.

The Russian commanding officer with his staff, who had taken over the Nazi camp commandant's house, sent for Dr. Baeck. When the elderly Rabbi entered the room where the officers were sitting, pitifully worn and thin, yet bearing himself with quiet dignity, they rose as one man to offer him a chair. And the Colonel, deeply moved, spoke to him in broken German. "We have come to help you," he said. "Help us to help you."

Doctors and nurses immunized against typhus were brought into the camp to care for the sick; and with them came drugs, nourishing food, and the first news from the outside to reach Theresienstadt for two years. Then plans were started to send back to their own countries the people who were well enough to travel.

The Russians thought that the Jews would want to have their revenge before they left. They had discovered in the camp a few frightened Germans, who had come there for safety after the guards had fled. These men the Russians offered to hand over to the Jews for punishment. But Dr. Baeck intervened with all his authority to prevent violence being done. However sorely his people had been tried, there must be no vengeance.

Immediately it was known that Dr. Baeck was still alive, arrangements were made to fly him to England; but he would not go until the camp was disbanded and all the survivors taken care of. On July 5th, nearly two months after the liberation, he left Germany for England: and at the London airport, waiting for him, was the daughter who had never ceased to hope that one day they might be reunited.

The prolonged ordeal through which he had passed had left Dr. Baeck very much shaken: but he was surprisingly strong, and those friends who feared to see a broken old man longing only for peace and rest were amazed when they found him looking old and thin, it is true, but otherwise unchanged. Very few Jewish leaders had survived in Germany and the Nazi-occupied countries of Europe, and there were many problems to be solved. Within a year of his release Dr. Baeck was in the thick of Jewish affairs. He was the leader and spokesman of the German Jews who had escaped the persecution and of the few who, like himself, had lived through it. He journeyed about Europe, helping to clear up the confusion the Nazis had left; and he founded a council of European Rabbis. He wrote; he lectured—more than once at the Hebrew University of Jerusalem; he was a very active president of the World Union for Progressive Judaism, the position he had courageously accepted in 1939. Among other causes, he served the Council of Christians and Jews, a body which exists to bring about good understanding between members of the two great religions. He had always been interested in Christianity, and while insistent on the underlying difference between Christianity and Judaism he liked to point out resemblances between them. When he attended a church service, as he sometimes did, he was especially moved to hear the priestly blessing which he spoke so often himself in synagogue: "The Lord bless you, and keep you: the Lord make his face to shine upon you, and be gracious unto you: the Lord lift up his countenance upon you, and give you peace."

There was no bitterness in Dr. Baeck's heart against the German people. He visited Germany several times, for there was much work for him to do there; and in 1953 on his eightieth birthday he accepted from the President of West Germany the award of the German Grand Order of Merit with Star. It was just ten years since the Nazis had sought to destroy his influence by sending him to Theresienstadt: now, in Germany, as in Europe and America, the true strength of that influence was recognized.

During the last years of his life Dr. Baeck spent the winter months in the United States. He had many friends in America—Einstein among them; but his chief reason for visiting America was to lecture at a training college for young rabbis in Cincinnati. On one of these visits his grand-daughter—now grown up—went with him; and in due course she married one of her grandfather's American students.

In February, 1948, the American House of Representatives invited Dr. Baeck to give the invocation prayer in Congress on the anniversary of Abraham Lincoln's birthday. He was the first non-American rabbi to receive this tribute; and he prayed for the American President who had championed the rights of the Negro people. In his prayer he spoke of " 'the man in whom is the spirit,' and who for the sake of this land became witness and testimony of humanity, herald of Thy command and Thy promise, to the everlasting blessing of this country and of mankind." Leo Baeck was thinking and speaking of Abraham Lincoln; but his words might equally well have been applied to himself.

Although he moved about so much, Dr. Baeck's real home was in England. As soon as possible he became a British subject; and he lived with his daughter in a London suburb. He had so many friends and admirers in England that he found it difficult to work, and used to disappear sometimes to a room he had rented to write and study. Nobody could disturb him then because the address of the room was known only to his daughter and his secretary. But he was far too friendly a man to want to disappear for long; and there are very many people in England today who remember the wise advice and help he gave them. Not that Dr. Baeck would have thought of it in that way: he always made a point of thanking other people for the help they gave him. Visitors from other countries also wanted to see him. One of the most distinguished was the great missionary doctor, Albert Schweitzer, who has given a lifetime of service to the people of Equatorial Africa. When the two men, who had served their fellow-men so well, met for the first time they had so much in common that they seemed like old friends.

Dr. Baeck lived until he was eighty-three, working and writing to the end. He lived long enough to see his first great-grandson grow from a baby to a four-year-old boy. Children of all ages were Dr. Baeck's friends. They liked him because he took them seriously; and they were never afraid of him although they sensed the authority in his quiet, gentle manner.

A short time before Dr. Baeck died his granddaughter brought her little son to England to see him; and although he was very weak, Dr. Baeck bent down to kiss the boy goodbye. On the first Sabbath eve after his death the boy— the son of a young rabbi, great-grandson of the most heroic rabbi of modern times—watched his grandmother light the candles and listened as she spoke the blessings. Then he took the bread-knife in his hand, saying as he cut the first slice of the Sabbath loaf: "This is a man's job, or at least a boy's."

CHAIM WEIZMANN
(1874-1952)
Israel's First President

WE have to go backwards in time now to the story of the
man who became the Zionist leader when Theodor
Herzl died. He was Chaim Weizmann, who had admired Herzl
but also opposed him. Fourteen years younger than
Herzl, Weizmann was the third of the fifteen children of
Oser Weizmann, twelve of whom lived to grow up. The
Weizmanns lived in the little town of Motol in the Pripet
Marshes of western Russia, and other members of the family
lived nearby.

As a child Chaim used to listen, fascinated, to the tales his
grandfather told him of the rabbis and heroes of Israel. The
story he liked best was of Sir Moses Montefiore's visit to
Russia; and he never tired of hearing how the Jews of Vilna
had welcomed their champion. When Sir Moses entered the
town they unharnessed the horses from his carriage and
dragged it in a procession through the streets. This was a
tribute which people through the ages have paid to the very
great.

Oser Weizmann was a timber merchant and his family was
well-to-do compared with most of the other Jewish families
of Motol. Oser owned his house and several acres of land on
which Rachel, his wife, kept chickens and two cows and grew
fruit and vegetables. Even so, with twelve children to be fed,

clothed and educated, there was never any money for luxuries.

Motol was within the Pale of Settlement beyond which the Jews were forbidden to live. Like the other Jewish children, Chaim went at the age of four to a *cheder*, a little Jewish school. The *cheder* had only one room, which was also occupied by the very incompetent teacher and his family. The room was generally festooned with washing, and the teacher's children rolled about the floor making as much noise as they wanted. In the long winter months the confusion was added to by a goat which took refuge from the cold in the schoolroom.

When he was eleven Chaim was sent with one of his brothers to a Russian high school in the nearby town of Pinsk, and he lodged with some friends of the family. As his father could not afford to pay the small lodging fees, Chaim found himself a job coaching a younger boy. The teaching in the school was poor: according to Chaim most of the teachers had turned to schoolmastering because they were not good enough for anything else. But one was outstandingly brilliant. He was the science master; and he had managed to form a small laboratory. He was the kind of teacher who inspires his pupils with his own enthusiasm; and to him Chaim Weizmann owed his own impulse towards the study of chemistry.

At eighteen the boy was ready for college. It was difficult for a Jew to enter a Russian university. Jewish candidates were given a specially difficult entrance examination, and even when they passed there was no guarantee that they would be accepted. Chaim therefore decided to go to Germany and he studied at the Universities of Berlin and Freiburg, where he gained the degrees of Doctor of Philosophy and Doctor of Science. By this time his family had moved from Motol to Pinsk; and when he could afford it Chaim went home during the vacations. All the other Weizmann children were now at school or college, and the house was always filled with their friends. They were a strange collection. Among them were Zionists, Socialists and revolutionaries; and they spent their evenings in endless argument. In the midst of the noise Mrs. Weizmann moved quietly between sitting-room and kitchen. She spent most of the time in the kitchen, preparing food. "They've got to be fed," she would say, "or they won't have the strength to shout."

Oser Weizmann was a Zionist; and as a boy Chaim had joined a branch of the Lovers of Zion in Pinsk. His first task was to collect money during the feast of Purim to help poor Jews to emigrate to Palestine. Purim fell during the thaws of late winter; and Chaim had to tramp the town from end to end in the mud and slush. To allow for growing his mother made his overcoats far too long, and sometimes he tripped over the hem and tumbled on his face in the mire. He would pick himself up and go on with his round; for his aim was to collect more money than anyone else. When he was older he visited the villages and small towns in the district, urging Jews to join the Lovers of Zion; to do all they could to help the cause of Zionism; and to appoint delegates to the first Zionist Congress. He himself was elected one of the delegates from Pinsk; and in gratitude for all the work he was doing for the cause, he was re-appointed year after year without an election.

Chaim Weizmann did not attend the first Congress. It was held during his second year at Berlin University, and he had recently made a small discovery which his professor thought he could sell in Moscow. Moscow lay beyond the Russian Pale, and a Jew entering the city without a special permit was liable to be arrested. Weizmann had no permit and so could not stay in an hotel. He was hidden by friends who would themselves have been arrested if he had been discovered. Nobody found him, and nobody would buy his discovery; but he stayed too long in Moscow to arrive in Basle before the Congress ended.

He went to the second Zionist Congress, however, saying very little but thinking deeply. Although, as we know, he found nothing new in Herzl's idea of a Jewish state, he was at home among the delegates, who were working on the same lines as he was; and he realized how important to the cause was Herzl's leadership.

These two leaders of the Zionist movement, Herzl the first, Weizmann the second, were entirely different. Herzl, dignified and handsome, with the polished manners and conversation which made him welcome in the courts of foreign rulers, was a Western European Jew, one of those who became drawn into the life of their country. Weizmann, a Russian Jew, who had grown up among his own people within the Pale, lacked Herzl's ease of manner. His face was full of intelligence, his eyes twinkled with humour; but he was not good-looking. His hair receded very early from his high square forehead; his features were strong rather than handsome; and his ears stuck out. While Herzl was gentle and courteous, Weizmann was forceful and inclined to be domineering, at any rate at the outset of his career. He made many enemies—as forceful people always do; but he had the charm of enthusiasm and utter sincerity, and his charm brought him many more friends than enemies. It also gave him authority when he spoke with politicians and statesmen. But although the two leaders had grown up under such very different conditions they were equally devoted to the cause of Zionism, and each of them served it with all his strength.

From his student days onwards Chaim Weizmann was conscious of a deep split within himself, a split between his love of Zionism and his love of science. He could not give either of them up; and it was to prove fortunate for Zionism that he did not wholly abandon his science. From the start he had shown remarkable brilliance as a chemist. There was no future for him in Russia, and when he had taken his doctorate he accepted a post as Lecturer in Chemistry at the University of Geneva. The appointment brought him nearer to the home of the Zionist movement; and during the three years he spent at Geneva he made his name both as a chemist and as a Zionist.

In Geneva he met a Russian-Jewish girl named Vera Chatzman. She was there to study medicine because, as a Jewess, she could not study in a Russian medical school.

There were seven years' difference between them: Chaim, a lecturer, was twenty-six, and Vera, a student was only nineteen. He was absorbed in his work for the Zionist cause; and, as yet, she knew little about it. But they grew to love one another very deeply and became engaged; and the girl began to make a thorough study of the subject which meant so much to him. In the meantime, they agreed not to marry until Vera had taken her medical degree.

After the fourth Zionist Congress, which did not lead, as Herzl had hoped, to an understanding with the Sultan of Turkey on the subject of Palestine, Weizmann and the other leading spirits among the Russian delegates formed a Zionist group of their own within the movement. They called it the "Democratic-Zionist Fraction"—or "the Fraction," for short; and it stood for an approach to the people rather than to rulers and princes, who might talk sympathetically but who did nothing. The Fraction appealed to the young men and women, the leaders of the future; and it stood for a revival in Palestine of Jewish learning and culture as well as a Jewish state. The Fraction was a very small group, numbering only thirty-seven; but it was exceedingly powerful, for its members always acted together, and so it had great influence on Congress debates. When it came to the question of a refuge for the Jews in East Africa, Weizmann and his friends—as we have seen—would not consider it for a moment. "With all their sufferings," wrote Weizmann, "the Jews of Russia were incapable of transferring their dreams and longings from the land of their forefathers to any other territory."

Herzl's early death caused a crisis in the Zionist movement. Those who believed that the first need was to establish a Jewish state somewhere in the world, though not necessarily in Palestine, broke away to form an organization of their own and to start a number of small Jewish farming communities in North and South America. The remainder (and they formed a big majority in the movement) continued the work begun by the Lovers of Zion, building and adding to the settlements in Palestine. The country had been neglected for centuries by its Arab inhabitants; but wherever a settlement was started Jewish farmers and labourers brought fertility back to the land.

In the year of Herzl's death Chaim Weizmann, now thirty years of age, decided to leave Switzerland and go to England. He felt, as Herzl had felt, that in England lay the hope of the future; and, for his own part, he had the strongest admiration for the country and its people. He knew very few people in England; he could speak scarcely a word of English; and he was aware that many of Herzl's Anglo-Jewish supporters thought that the Russian delegates' opposition to the East Africa plan was the cause of the strain and anxiety which hastened their leader's death. Weizmann felt sure that the Jews of London would treat him as an outcast; and so he went to Manchester, which had a large chemical industry, with a university famed for its medical school.

He knew only one person in Manchester, a Zionist, who was a printer by trade and a Hebrew poet by choice. This man took him into his own home until he could find lodgings. He also introduced him to Charles Dreyfus, the chairman of the Manchester Zionist Society. Dreyfus was managing director of a big chemical works; and he gave the penniless Weizmann some research work to do.

One of the Geneva professors had given Weizmann an introduction to his opposite number at Manchester University; and as a result he was allowed the use of a laboratory. It was in a dark and dirty basement; and Dr. Weizmann spent his first day scrubbing, cleaning and washing the apparatus. The next day, armed with an English chemistry textbook, he began to puzzle out its meaning with the help of the laboratory steward. He was also allocated a lab. boy, who had a mania for football. The boy never passed him anything—even the most delicate piece of glass—in the ordinary way. He always slung or kicked it; but with such care and precision that it landed exactly where it was needed.

It soon became clear that Dr. Weizmann had something to offer the University in the way of chemical discovery; and he was invited to give a weekly lecture to students on some branch of chemistry. His English, though much better than when he arrived, was still far from good; and the idea of lecturing in English made him extremely nervous. When he entered the theatre for the first time he took the students into his confidence. He was a foreigner, he told them, who had been in the country only a few months. He would do his best, but he was bound to make howlers. After the lecture the audience could laugh as much as they liked; but he hoped they would give him a fair hearing. They listened in silence; and when the lecture was over they showed their appreciation by staying to discuss its chief points and ask questions. Dr. Weizmann was never nervous again. His lectures were a great success and led to more work for the University. Later on he was appointed to the staff, as Reader in Biochemistry.

In 1906, when he had been two years in Manchester, Dr. Weizmann met a future Prime Minister, the man who was to offer, on behalf of his Government, a national home for the Jews in Palestine. He was Arthur James Balfour, Conservative Parliamentary candidate for one of the Manchester divisions; and Weizmann was introduced to him by Charles Dreyfus, who was chairman of the Manchester Conservative Association.

Mr. Balfour opened the conversation by asking Dr. Weizmann why it was that some Jews refused to have anything to do with the offer of a refuge in East Africa. He could not have asked a better question; and Dr. Weizmann, in reply, sought to convince him of the inner meaning of Zionism; the unshakable conviction that only in Zion could the Jews as a people find their real home. If, he said, Moses had come back to earth and had listened to the debate that ended in a resolution that the East African offer should at least be considered, he would have broken the stone tablets of the Law once again. To the Zionist, he added, no country could possibly have the appeal of Palestine; and in no other country could the Jews build and work as they would in the land of their forefathers. He finished by asking: "Mr. Balfour, supposing I were to offer you Paris instead of London, would you take it?" "But, Dr. Weizmann," Mr.

Balfour answered in surprise, "we have London." "That is true. But we had Jerusalem when London was a marsh." Mr. Balfour did not forget this conversation; but nothing could be done about it at the time.

It was in 1906—the year of this meeting—that Chaim Weizmann's marriage to Vera Chatzman took place; and the newly married couple settled in Manchester. Vera Weizmann had taken an excellent medical degree; she spoke four languages and was a fine pianist. She was an altogether charming young woman; but of housekeeping she knew nothing at all. The first thing that baffled her was the arrival of the butcher's boy asking for orders. "I want meat," was all she could say; for she had no idea that she was expected to name the animal and the cut of meat she wanted.

But she was willing to learn, and with the help of the wives of her husband's colleagues she soon became an excellent housekeeper. She was, too, the perfect wife for a man who was both scientist and Zionist leader; and to her he owed all the happiness of a busy, stormy life. Before long the Weizmanns' first son, Benjamin (called Benjy, for short) was born; and as soon as they could afford a nurse for the baby, Mrs. Weizmann studied for her English medical degree and took a post as medical officer under the Manchester Department of Health.

In Manchester Dr. Weizmann became the central figure in the Zionist movement; for he gathered round himself a group of enthusiastic, hard-working British Zionists. One of them—a leader writer on the influential *Manchester Guardian*—introduced him to his famous Editor, C. P. Scott, and to another well-known journalist, Herbert Sidebotham. Scott and Sidebotham were very sympathetic towards Zionism; and they championed Weizmann's ideas in print. They also arranged for him to meet some of the politicians of the day, including another future Prime Minister, David Lloyd George.

People who knew Dr. Weizmann well recall that he was at his finest when he spoke on equal terms with statesmen like Lloyd George and A. J. Balfour. Chaim Weizmann ("a Yid from Motol," as he sometimes laughingly called himself) possessed the genius of a great statesman, and although he could be impatient and domineering with lesser men, on the highest level his genius was understood.

During his Manchester days Weizmann's original dream of a revival of education and culture in Palestine was merged with Herzl's idea of a political Jewish state; so that the two ideas became one. But Dr. Weizmann continued to look to the creation of a Hebrew university as the goal of those Russian Jews who, like himself, could not attend a Russian university. To his great happiness, it was agreed at the Zionist Congress of 1911 to found such a university. An estate was bought on Mount Scopus, above Jerusalem. In 1914 war broke out between Britain and her allies, and Germany and *her* allies, including Turkey. Although the war hindered building, Dr. Weizmann laid the foundation stones of the Hebrew University in the summer of 1918, while fighting in the Middle East against Turkey was still going on. It was a simple ceremony but a very impressive one. "The declining sun flooded the hills of Judea and Moab with golden light," he wrote, "and it seemed to me, too, that the transfigured heights were watching, wondering, dimly aware perhaps that this was the beginning of the return of their own people after many days."

By 1918 there was reason to believe that "the beginning of the return" was in sight. It was a move in which Dr. Weizmann had himself been involved. He had become a British subject some years before war with Germany started; and at the outbreak he was summoned to the Admiralty in London and offered the position of Director of the Admiralty Laboratories. He was told that the country was suffering from a grave shortage of acetone, which was used in the making of high explosives. "Well, Dr. Weizmann," said the First Lord of the Admiralty, Mr. (now Sir) Winston Churchill, "we need thirty thousand tons of acetone. Can you make it?" Dr. Weizmann was so alarmed at this tremendous demand that he almost turned tail and fled; but, instead, he answered that with Government backing he would do all he could. A laboratory was built for him; and he moved from Manchester to London, where his wife and Benjy joined him. The Weizmanns made up their minds to settle in London, and in 1917 their second son, Michael, was born there.

Meanwhile, despite the difficulty of getting raw materials in wartime, Dr. Weizmann had succeeded in discovering a new way of producing acetone. The discovery undoubtedly helped Britain to win the war; and it made certain British statesmen feel that they could best repay the inventor by helping him to realize his dream. Chief among these statesmen was A. J. Balfour, whom Weizmann had first met in 1906. "Well," said Mr. Balfour when the two men met for the second time in 1917, "you haven't changed much." And almost without a pause he added: "You know, I was thinking of that conversation of ours, and I believe that when the guns stop firing you may get your Jerusalem."

On November 2nd, 1917, Balfour—then Britain's Foreign Secretary—issued a declaration which stated that the British Government viewed "with favour" the establishment in Palestine of a National Home for the Jewish people; and would do what they could to bring it about. It must be clearly understood, however, that nothing should be done to interfere with the rights of the non-Jewish communities in Palestine, or the rights of Jews living in other countries.

This statement—known as the Balfour Declaration—was hailed with tremendous excitement by Zionists in all parts of the world. Many of them imagined that within a few months, or a few years at most, there would be a general return of the Jewish people to the land of their origin.

By no means all Jews were Zionists. Some feared that whatever the terms of the Declaration, the establishment of a Jewish home would damage the position of Jews who continued to live in other countries. Some Jews like Leo Baeck believed that the Jews were not an ordinary nation but a religious people. Scattered as they were over the world, they could be as faithful to their Judaism as ever they could be in Palestine. And they remembered the message which

Moses had given the Children of Israel in the name of their God: "And ye shall be unto me a kingdom of priests, and an holy nation."

To the Zionists, the meaning of the Balfour Declaration was clear: a Jewish state in Palestine with full political rights would be created: it would be a country as independent as Britain herself. There were many Jews, however, who did not think that a National Home necessarily meant an independent state. To them, the meaning of the Declaration was not clear: it might mean a state; or it might simply mean a large settlement of Jews under the protection of Britain or some other country.

The terms of the Balfour Declaration had been quickly confirmed by the Governments of Britain's allies; and this encouraged Jews to believe that their National Home would soon come into being. The war years had been a time of especial sorrow to them; for some had fought on Britain's side and some on Germany's. The members of, say, a German-Jewish family who had settled in England before the war and become British subjects naturally fought for Britain; but members of the same family who had remained in Germany fought on the German side. Yet each man fought as a loyal citizen of his country, and old family ties had to be forgotten.

In Palestine itself, Jewish settlers numbered more than 100,000 by 1914. They lived and worked in the farming settlements (or *kibbutzim*) and also in the towns. Sir Moses Montefiore, on one of his visits to Palestine, had suggested building outside the city of Jerusalem; and now Jews were putting up houses which in due course were to form Jerusalem's new city; while building had also been started at Tel-Aviv, the first all-Jewish city.

During the war the Palestinian Jews worked and fought for Britain. Many served in the Allied armies: some joined the special Jewish battalions (one of them was made up entirely of American volunteers) which were formed in England and went to Palestine to help in the final drive for victory. The war finished in the autumn of 1918; it put an end to the Turkish Empire and Turkey's long rule over the Middle East.

In Russia, Britain's ally until 1917, the Bolshevik Revolution which broke out that autumn led at first to civil war and to renewed suffering for the Jews. They were accused, without reason, of treachery by the forces of the old Russia and the forces of the new; and massacres occurred in towns and villages as dreadful as any that had occurred in the past. Distress and disorder continued until the new Government was firmly in control. Under Soviet rule, which promised equality to Jews as to all other Russian subjects, many Jews felt hopeful and secure. But thousands more, fearing that they would be squeezed out of the new Russia and the new Poland, which was formed after the war from parts of Russia, Germany and Austria, fled from Eastern Europe. They went to Canada, South America, and particularly to the United States; and over the years the flight from Eastern Europe provided the United States with the largest Jewish population of any country in the world.

Inevitably, there were Jews who turned with longing towards Palestine. Early in 1918, some months before the end of the war, the British Government sent a Zionist Commission to Palestine to find out all they could about how the terms of the Balfour Declaration could best be realized, and also to act as a link between the Jews of Palestine and the British authorities. The Commission was headed by Dr. Weizmann; and it was while he was in Palestine that he laid the foundation stones of the Hebrew University. Seven years later the University was opened: the ceremony was presided over by Dr. Weizmann; and the chief speaker was A. J. (by now Lord) Balfour, an old man and a true friend to learning and to Zionism.

At the Peace Conference which was held after the war Dr. Weizmann led the delegation which put forward the Zionist claims. The Conference took place at a time of grave anxiety about the fate of the Jews of Eastern Europe; and the more ardent and impetuous Zionists thought that Dr. Weizmann was a great deal too reasonable and modest in his demands. But Dr. Weizmann was well aware that the situation was extremely difficult and tricky; and that claims were also being made on behalf of the vast Arab population of the Middle East. His own hopes were pinned on the creation of a Jewish National Home; but he realized, as his more hot-headed followers did not, that it could not be created by violence. In his demands and requests Dr. Weizmann had taught himself only to use the moderation and tolerance of a statesman; for he knew that in this way he would in the end gain more. But in the years to come his wise moderation often made him unpopular with the extreme Zionists. To the majority of his followers, however, he was a great leader. They might disagree with him, but they trusted him. And they trusted him not only because of his leadership but also because he was as Jewish as they were.

The future of Palestine was decided not by Britain but by the League of Nations, which was founded in January 1920 with the object of maintaining peace and security in the world. The League entrusted to Britain the Mandate for Palestine: that is to say, the country was to be governed by Britain until such time as the people were ready to govern themselves.

In the same year Dr. Weizmann was elected President of the Executive of the World Zionist Organization. This made him the official leader of the movement and the spokesman of Zionism. He was the man to whom Zionists all over the world looked to build the National Home which the Balfour Declaration had promised.

In Palestine, plans were immediately made to organize farming and industry on a very large scale; to deal with such questions as health and education; to prepare the way for vast numbers of Jews to enter the country. In 1923, after three years under military government, the normal form of government was set up headed by a High Commissioner representing King George V. The first High Commissioner of Palestine was a Jew, Sir Herbert (later Viscount) Samuel, a man who had held high office in the British Government, who sympathized with Dr. Weizmann's hopes and who, like him, longed to see the establishment of a Jewish National Home. In Jerusalem, an organization called the Jewish Agency was established a few years later, with Dr. Weizmann as its leading spirit. Its members were elected from among the leaders of world Jewry; and it acted as a link between the Government and the Jewish population.

The chief problem which faced the Government was how to put the Balfour Declaration into effect without making enemies of the Arabs, both inside Palestine and in the surrounding Arab states. The Jewish Agency felt that too much partiality was being shown to the Arabs: but as more and more Jews entered Palestine, the Arabs became increasingly restive and hostile. The Agency tried to bring the Jews and the Arabs together: but the Arabs refused to work with the Jews. In the end they declared that they would not recognize the existence of a Jewish National Home, and they demanded that the Balfour Declaration be withdrawn.

The Government, trying to keep the peace and treat Jews and Arabs alike with justice, made mistakes and was accused of injustice by both sides. The task of governing the country became even harder after 1933 when German Jews began to flee from the terrible menace of Adolf Hitler. The number entering Palestine naturally grew very swiftly; and the increase made the Arabs fearful that they would be swamped and driven out by the Jews.

In 1936 Arab resistance flared into open revolt; and the following year the British Government put forward a plan for the division (or partition) of Palestine into a small Jewish state and an Arab state. There would not be room in the Jewish state, the Government statement declared, for an enormous Jewish population, and so the number of immigrants was to be restricted.

Dr. Weizmann believed that even with a small Jewish state partition was the best solution. But he was quite unprepared for the blow struck by the British Government in the spring of 1939. Despite Arab fears, the tide of Jewish immigration had continued to increase. And now, in a

Government White Paper, it was laid down that when 75,000 more immigrants had entered Palestine, no more Jews would be allowed in without Arab consent. The White Paper also laid it down that at the end of ten years an independent state should be established in Palestine. The state would be made up of Jews and Arabs, but the Arabs should form two-thirds of the population, and the Jews only one-third. The Jews were not prepared to accept this division: and desperate fugitives began to enter the country secretly and by unlawful means.

The White Paper was severely criticized in the British House of Commons. Mr. Churchill was among the Members of Parliament who attacked it for its injustice towards the Jews. He called it "a plain breach of a solemn obligation;" while a Socialist leader, Mr. Herbert Morrison, spoke of it as "a cynical breach of pledges given to the Jews and the world, including America."

To Zionists all over the world the White Paper was like a death blow. But by the time the Zionist Congress met at Geneva in August, 1939, world war had drawn very near. "Of course," wrote Dr. Weizmann, "we rejected the White Paper unanimously." Yet, despite the bitterness it aroused, he went on, "our protest against the White Paper ran parallel with our solemn declaration that in the coming world struggle we stood committed more than any other people in the world to the defence of democracy and therefore to co-operation with England—author of the White Paper."

Both Dr. Weizmann's sons joined the British fighting services; and to his parents' grief Michael, the younger, was killed in 1942 while serving in the R.A.F. The Weizmanns were still living in London, but during the war they made several trips to America in connection with the scientific work which Dr. Weizmann was once more doing for the British Government. He also spoke to American Jewish scientists, urging them to take an interest in the scientific work which had been started in Palestine.

Dr. Weizmann's post in the second world war was honorary Chemical Adviser to the Ministry of Supply. He had a tiny laboratory and the help of a small group of scientists. There was an air-raid shelter attached to the laboratory; but because they hated to interrupt their work, Dr. Weizmann and his group did not use the shelter during the bombing of London. Had they done so they would certainly have been killed; for in one of the raids the shelter received a direct hit and was completely smashed. The work they were doing was the invention of substances to replace products of which there was a wartime shortage, such as rubber and aviation fuel; and Dr. Weizmann, who found it absorbing, was glad to be doing something to help the war effort. But his thoughts returned again and again to Palestine. He knew that nothing could be done until the war was over; but he was greatly comforted to realize that in Britain Mr. Churchill—by now Prime Minister—and in America the President, Mr. Roosevelt, sympathized with the Zionist aims.

As the facts became known of the terrible tragedy which had overwhelmed the Jews of Germany and German-occupied Europe, it became clear that if any of them survived Palestine would be their chief goal. But by the end of the war in 1945 the White Paper had not been officially withdrawn; and there was still a ban on Jews entering the country. Nevertheless, Jews were still contriving to get in, using their secret, illegal means, and helped by the Jewish population of Palestine.

The Arabs, more hostile than ever, had been making frequent small raids on Jewish settlements and to ward off these attacks the Jews had formed their own armed force, *Hagganah*. But violent, extremist Zionist groups were also formed; and they launched terrorist attacks on Arabs and British officials and soldiers.

There were some Zionists who thought that, in the face of injustice, terrorism and murder were justified. Dr. Weizmann was not among them. He was called weak; but he refused to countenance terrorist methods; and the moderate Zionists thought as he did. " 'Thou shalt not kill,' " he said, "has been ingrained in us since Mount Sinai." And he felt shame that Jews should break this Commandment. "Unfortunately, they are breaking it today," he went on, "and nobody deplores it more than the vast majority of the Jews."

Outside Palestine, particularly in Britain, terrorism led to some anti-Jewish feeling. The future looked very dark when the British Government invited the Government of the United States to join them in consultations. The outcome of their talks was that the whole problem of Palestine was turned over to the United Nations, the organization which had taken the place of the old League of Nations. The United Nations worked out a new scheme for partition. Under it, the Jews would have a small state, the Arabs another; and the city of Jerusalem would become an international zone. On November 27th, 1947, after a vote in the United Nations Assembly, it was declared that the Mandate for Palestine should be brought to an end as soon as possible: in its place two independent states, one Jewish, one Arab, should come into being. The Zionists agreed to the decision reluctantly. The Jewish state was very small, and open to Arab attack. But at least it would be independent, free to admit every Jew who wished to enter. The Arabs, on the other hand, rejected the decision. They began to recruit a huge army to prevent the enforcement of partition; and they made no secret of the fact that they intended to drive the Jews out of Palestine by force.

Britain, committed to the United Nations' decision, simply withdrew from Palestine on May 14th, 1948, leaving the country at the mercy of the opposing sides. At once, the Jewish State of Israel was proclaimed. It was a small state and a vulnerable one; but its citizens, men and women, would fight to the death to defend it.

Wasting no time, the Arab army, backed by the surrounding Arab states, launched an attack on the Israeli forces: but the Israeli Army stood firm. The Arabs, though strong in numbers, were poorly prepared for war; while the Israeli Army, stiffened by Palestinian Jews who had fought on Britain's side in the war, remained unbeaten. When the brief fighting came to an end, the Arab Army had been routed, and the frontiers of Israel had been strengthened and extended.

News of the proclamation of the State of Israel reached Dr. Weizmann in America. He was not very well, and was resting after the excitement of the announcement, when a message was brought to him that the Provisional Council of State, meeting at Tel-Aviv, had elected him President of Israel. He thought it was only a rumour, for, with an invasion on their hands, the Council must have many more urgent problems to solve. A few hours later the message was repeated on the radio; but he had to wait until the next day to hear the details. He learned then that his election had been proposed by the Minister of Justice and seconded by the Prime Minister and Minister of Defence, Mr. David Ben-Gurion. "I doubt whether the Presidency is necessary to Dr. Weizmann," Mr. Ben-Gurion had said, "but the Presidency of Dr. Weizmann is a moral necessity for the State of Israel."

Chaim Weizmann was an old man now, tired, nearly blind, and in bad health: but there was no question in his mind that he must take on this new duty, and so he accepted. He gave his first address as President in the *Knesset*—the Israeli Parliament—in the modern part of Jerusalem which had stayed in Israeli hands after the Arab attack. In his speech he spoke of peace and of his hope for the future. "From this eternal city of Jerusalem a message of hope and good cheer goes forth to the world. From this sacred place we send our fraternal blessings to our brethren in the four corners of the earth. We stretch out the hand of hope to the neighbouring countries, of friendship to all peace-loving people in the world."

In the following year, on August 17th, a ceremony was held in the presence of members of the Israeli Government and of thousands of the people. A coffin containing the remains of Theodor Herzl was brought by air from Vienna, and it was buried where Herzl had most longed to lie, in the soil of Palestine. His resting-place, on a hill to the west of Jerusalem, was named Mount Herzl in his honour. And, because he had wished it, the remains of his sister Pauline were also given a final resting place in Israel.

To President Weizmann, the new State was a great joy and a great responsibility. He lived to see Israel open her gates to all those Jews who yearned to make it their home: and he looked towards the future in the hope that an era of lasting peace would succeed the troubled years of the present. When he died, in the autumn of 1952, people from all parts of Israel flocked to pay him homage in the little town of Rehovot where he had lived. And before the funeral service began sirens wailed throughout the country, the signal for a two-minutes silence in remembrance of the man who had brought his people home. Among the many messages of sympathy sent to the Prime Minister and to Mrs. Weizmann was one from Dr. Weizmann's old friend Sir Winston Churchill. "The world has lost a distinguished citizen and Israel a faithful son," he wrote.

If the era of lasting peace to which Dr. Weizmann looked still lies ahead, in the ten years which have passed since the State was proclaimed Israel has made friends among the nations; and, despite all the problems which beset her, has found room for a Jewish population which now numbers nearly a million-and-a-half. To Jews all over the world, to Zionists—and to many who are not Zionists—Israel stands today for the dignity and freedom of the country which their ancestors owned and lost, but which is theirs once more.

INDEX

Printed in Great Britain by
The Camelot Press Ltd, London and Southampton
for Abelard-Schuman Ltd, 38 Russell Square, London, WC1
and 404 Fourth Avenue, New York 16, NY